AF477150

Common data model for the S-Series IPS Specifications

SX002D-B6865-0X000-00

Issue No. 2.1

Usage rights: Refer to SX002D-A-00-00-0000-00A-021A-A.

Copyright (C) 2021 by each of the following organizations

– AeroSpace and Defence Industries Association of Europe - ASD

Publishers:

AeroSpace and Defence
Industries Association of Europe

Aerospace Industries
Association of America

Applicable to: All   SX002D-A-00-00-0000-00A-001A-A

This specification has been developed by the following organizations (in alphabetic order):

- Airbus Defense & Space   Spain & Germany
- HiCo   Austria
- ISS   United States of America
- Isselnord   Italy
- Nexter Group   France
- Rolls-Royce   United Kingdom
- Pentecom   United States of America
- Saab AB   Sweden
- Sopra Steria   Germany

Editor:
- O'Neil & Associates   United States of America

The following people contributed to the development of this specification (in alphabetic order):

- AUGSBURGER, Ryan
- DAY, Mike
- DE LANGE, Daan
- FLECK, Andreas
- GAMEZ DE LA FUENTE, Daniel
- GYLLSTROM, Leif #
- HASLAM, Paul +
- MITJANS, Félix *
- OWEN, Parker
- PINTER, Andreas
- SOMOZA, Ramón
- TEDESCHI, Stefano

*= Chair   #= Former Chair   += Editor-in-Chief

ISBN: 978-84-19125-24-8

Published 2022 in book format by Editorial Dragón with permission of the AeroSpace and Defence Industries Association of Europe – ASD

PDF publisher – O'Neil & Associates

Highlights

The following tables summarize the changes that brought about changes to the chapters highlighted. Table 1 lists changes that are common to many chapters.

List of tables

Table 1 Summary

CPF	Summary of changes
N/A	The specification introduces 14 new Unit of Functionality (UoF). These UoF have been added to Chapter 3 in alphabetical order which means that most UoF have been assigned new chapter numbers
	The term Integrated Logistics Support (ILS) has been changed to Integrated Product Support (IPS). This change has been introduced to all S-Series IPS specifications

Table 2 Chap 1

Chap No.	Summary of changes
Chap 1.3	The business-oriented data model, using UML class models to define Units of Functionality (UoF), has been updated. 14 new UoF has been added. The suggested order, in which the UoF definitions should be read, has been updated accordingly

Table 3 Chap 2

Chap No.	Summary of changes
Chap 2.2	A short description for each compound attribute has been added
Chap 2.3	The S-Series base object have an additional attribute `uri` which provides the capability to uniquely identify an instance of an UML class in the context of the World Wide Web

Table 4 Chap 3

Chap No.	Summary of changes
Chap 3.3	New UoF Analysis candidate item
Chap 3.4	UoF Applicability statement has been moved from Chapter 3.3 to Chapter 3.4 The following is renamed: - The `ConditionTypeAssertMember` attribute `assertValueRelationalOperator` has been renamed

Chap No.	Summary of changes

conditionTypeAssertMemberAssertValueComparisonOperator

Other changes:

- The number of classes that realizes the `ApplicabilityStatementItem` <<extend>> interface has been extended

Chap 3.5

UoF Breakdown structure has been moved from Chapter 3.4 to Chapter 3.5

The following attributes has been added:

- Attribute `breakdownRevisionRationale` and `breakdownRevisionDate` to `BreakdownRevision`
- Attribute `breakdownElementChildSequenceNumber` to `BreakdownElementStructure`
- Attribute `breakdownElementDescription`, `breakdownElementRevisionRationale` and `breakdownElementRevisionDate` to `BreakdownElementRevision`

Other changes:

- `BreakdownRevisionRelationship` has been added to allow for instances of `BreakdownRevision` to refer to other instances of `BreakdownRevision`

Chap 3.6

New UoF Capability definition

Chap 3.7

UoF Change information has been moved from Chapter 3.5 to Chapter 3.7

The following change has been introduced:

- The number of classes that realizes the `ChangeControlledItem` <<extend>> interface has been extended

Chap 3.8

New UoF Circuit breaker

This UoF adds to the definition of circuit breakers, previously part of UoF Task (refer to Chap 3.39)

The following changes have been introduced:

- Further characterizations can now be provided for a circuit breaker location by the introduction of the `CircuitBreakerLocation` class
- The `CircuitBreakerLocation` <<select>> interface has been renamed `CircuitBreakerLocationItem`
- The number of classes that realizes the `CircuitBreakerLocationItem` <<select>> interface has been extended

Chap 3.9

UoF Competence definition has been moved from Chapter 3.6 to Chapter 3.9

Chap 3.10

New UoF Damage definition

Chap 3.11

New UoF Decision tree template definition

Chap 3.12

UoF Design change request has been moved from Chapter 3.7 to Chapter 3.12

The following change has been introduced:

- The number of classes that realizes the `ChangeRequestRationaleItem` <<extend>> interface has been extended

Chap 3.13

UoF Digital file has been moved from Chapter 3.8 to Chapter 3.13

The following changes has been introduced:

- The number of classes that realizes the `DigitalFileReferencingItem`

Chap No.	Summary of changes

	<<extend>> interface has been extended
	- The number of classes that realizes the `DigitalFileReferencedItem` <<select>> interface has been extended
Chap 3.14	UoF Document has been moved from Chapter 3.9 to Chapter 3.14 The following attributes has been added: - Attribute `documentIssueRationale` and `documentIssueStatus` to `DocumentIssue` Other changes: - Explicit composition associations have been added between `S1000DDataModule` and `S1000DDataModuleIssue` - Explicit composition associations have been added between `S1000DPublicationModule` and `S1000DPublicationModuleIssue`
Chap 3.15	New UoF Environment definition
Chap 3.16	UoF Facility has been moved from Chapter 3.10 to Chapter 3.16 The following changes has been introduced: - `FacilityRelationship` has been added to allow for instances of Facility to refer to other instances of `Facility` - `FacilityLocation` has been added to allow for a `Facility` to have different locations over time
Chap 3.17	New UoF Failure mode
Chap 3.18	UoF Hardware element has been moved from Chapter 3.11 to Chapter 3.18
Chap 3.19	New UoF In service optimization analysis
Chap 3.20	UoF Location has been moved from Chapter 3.12 to Chapter 3.20 The following change has been introduced: - `County` has been defined as a class and is no longer just an attribute of `StreetAddress`
Chap 3.21	New UoF Measurement point This UoF has been added to better illustrate that instances of `MeasurementPoint` can be defined in multiple contexts. It was previously part of UoF Part as realized (refer to Chap 3.25)
Chap 3.22	UoF Message has been moved from Chapter 3.13 to Chapter 3.22
Chap 3.23	New UoF Mission definition
Chap 3.24	UoF Organization has been moved from Chapter 3.14 to Chapter 3.24
Chap 3.25	UoF Part as realized has been moved from Chapter 3.15 to Chapter 3.25 The following have been renamed: - Class `ModificationOf` has been renamed `SerializedHardwarePartModification` and its attribute `modificationDate` has been renamed `serializedHardwarePartModificationDate` Other changes: - The representation of `MeasurementPoint` has been moved to the UoF

Chap No.	Summary of changes
	Measurement point (refer to Chap 3.21)
Chap 3.26	UoF Part definition has been moved from Chapter 3.16 to Chapter 3.26 The following attributes has been added: – Attribute `partsListRevisionRationale` and `partsListRevisionDate` to `PartAsDesignedPartsListRevision`
Chap 3.27	New UoF Performance parameter
Chap 3.28	UoF Product and project has been moved from Chapter 3.17 to Chapter 3.28 The following have been renamed: – Class `ContractItemDetails` attribute `quantityOfContractItem` has been renamed `contractItemDetailsContractQuantity`
Chap 3.29	UoF Product design configuration has been moved from Chapter 3.18 to Chapter 3.29
Chap 3.30	UoF Product usage context has been moved from Chapter 3.19 to Chapter 3.30
Chap 3.31	New UoF Product usage phase
Chap 3.32	UoF Remark has been moved from Chapter 3.20 to Chapter 3.32
Chap 3.33	New UoF Resource specification This UoF adds to the definition of resource specifications, previously part of UoF Task resource (refer to Chap 3.41) The following changes have been introduced: – `ResourceSpecificationRevision` has been added to allow for better traceability of `ResourceSpecification` over time – Instances of `ResourceSpecification` can now be categorized using the `resourceSpecificationType` attribute
Chap 3.34	UoF Security classification has been moved from Chapter 3.21 to Chapter 3.34 The following changes have been introduced: – The attribute `securityClassificationAuthority` has been added to `SecurityClassification` – The number of classes that realizes the `SecurityClassificationItem` <<extend>> interface has been extended
Chap 3.35	UoF Serialized part configuration has been moved from Chapter 3.22 to Chapter 3.35
Chap 3.36	UoF Serialized product variant configuration has been moved from Chapter 3.23 to Chapter 3.36 The following change has been introduced: – The association with `MeasurementPoint` has been moved to the UoF Measurement point (refer to Chap 3.21)
Chap 3.37	UoF Software element has been moved from Chapter 3.24 to Chapter 3.37
Chap 3.38	New UoF Special event
Chap 3.39	UoF Task has been moved from Chapter 3.25 to Chapter 3.39 The following attributes has been added:

Chap No.	Summary of changes

- Attribute `taskRevisionRationale` and `taskRevisionDate` to `TaskRevision`

Other changes:

- The representation of `CircuitBreaker` and its location has been moved to the UoF Circuit breaker (refer to Chap 3.8)

Chap 3.40

UoF Task requirement has been moved from Chapter 3.26 to Chapter 3.40

The following have been renamed:

- Class `TaskRequirementRevision` attribute `taskRequirementDate` has been renamed `taskRequirementRevisionDate`

The following attributes has been added:

- Attribute `taskRequirementRevisionRationale` to `TaskReuqirementRevision`

Other changes:

- `TaskRequirementJustification` and `TaskRequirementJustificationItem` has been added to the UoF

Chap 3.41

UoF Task resources has been moved from Chapter 3.27 to Chapter 3.41

The following change has been introduced:

- All specializations of `TaskInfrastructureResource` and `TaskMaterialResource` has been deleted and their associations with `ResourceSpecification`, `PartAsDesigned`, `PartAsDesignedPartsListEntry` and `BreakdownElement` has been replaced by the new `TaskResourceDefinitionItem` <<select>> interface
- The detailed representation of `ResourceSpecification` has been moved to the UoF Resource specification (refer to Chap 3.33)

Chap 3.42   UoF Task usage has been moved from Chapter 3.28 to Chapter 3.42

Chap 3.43   UoF Time limit has been moved from Chapter 3.29 to Chapter 3.43

Chap 3.44   UoF Zone element has been moved from Chapter 3.30 to Chapter 3.44

Applicable to: All

Page intentionally blank.

End of data module

Copyright and user agreement

1   Copyright

Copyright (C) 2021 by AeroSpace and Defence Industries Association of Europe (ASD).

All rights reserved. No part of this document may be reproduced or transmitted in any form or by any means, electronic or mechanical, including photocopying and recording, or by any information storage or retrieval system, except as may be expressly permitted by the Copyright Act or in writing by the Publisher.

SX002D® is an in EU registered trademark owned by ASD.

All correspondence and queries should be directed to:

ASD
10 Rue Montoyer
B-1000 Brussels
Belgium

2   Agreement for use of the SX002D™ suite of information

2.1   Definitions

The **SX002D™ suite of information** means, but is not limited to:

- the common data model specification SX002D
- SX002D XML schemas
- SX002D UML model
- any other related software or information on the page titled " Downloads" on the website www.sx000i.org

Copyright Holder means ASD.

2.2   Notice to user

By using all or any portion of the **SX002D™ suite of information** you accept the terms and conditions of this copyright and user agreement.

This copyright and user agreement is enforceable against you and any legal entity that has obtained the **SX002D ™ suite of information** or any portion thereof and on whose behalf it is used.

2.3   License to use

As long as you comply with the terms of this User Agreement, , then the Copyright Holder grant to you a non-exclusive license to use the **SX002D ™ suite of information**.

2.4   Intellectual property rights

The **SX002D ™ suite of information** is the intellectual property of, and is owned by, the Copyright Holder and AIA. Except as expressly stated herein, this Copyright and user User Agreement does not grant you any intellectual property right in the **SX002D ™ suite of information** and all rights not expressly granted are reserved by the Copyright Holders

2.5   No modifications

You must not modify, adapt or translate, in whole or in part, the **SX002D ™ suite of information**. You can however add business rules and/or tailor it to suit the needs of your project.

2.6 No warranty

The **SX002D ™ suite of information** is being delivered to you "as is". The Copyright Holder do not warrant the performance or result you may obtain by using the **SX002D ™ suite of information**. The Copyright Holder make no warranties, representations or indemnities, express or implied, whether by statute, common law, custom, usage or otherwise as to any matter including without limitation merchantability, integration, satisfactory quality, fitness for any particular purpose, or non-infringement of third parties rights.

2.7 Limitation of liability

In no event will the Copyright Holder be liable to you for any damages, claims or costs whatsoever or any consequential, indirect or incidental damages, or any lost profits or lost savings or for any claim by a third party, even if the Copyright Holder have been advised of the possibility of such damages, claims, costs, lost profits or lost savings.

2.8 Indemnity

You agree to defend, indemnify, and hold harmless the Copyright Holder and its parent and affiliates and all of their employees, agents, directors, officers, proprietors, partners, representatives, shareholders, servants, attorneys, predecessors, successors, assigns, and those who have worked on the preparation, publication or distribution of the **SX002D ™ suite of information** from and against any and all claims, proceedings, damages, injuries, liabilities, losses, costs, and expenses (including reasonable attorneys' fees and litigation expenses), relating to or arising from your use of the **SX002D ™ suite of information** or any breach by you of this copyright and user agreement.

2.9 Governing law

This copyright and user agreement will be governed by and construed in accordance with the laws of the Kingdom of Belgium.

In the event of any dispute, controversy or claim arising out of or, in connection with, this Copyright and User Agreement, or the breach, termination or invalidity thereof, the parties agree to submit the matter to settlement proceedings under the ICC (International Chamber of Commerce) Alternative Dispute Resolution (ADR) rules. If the dispute has not been settled pursuant to the said rules within 45 days following the filing of a request for ADR or within such other period as the parties may agree in writing, such dispute shall be finally settled under the rules of arbitration of the ICC by three arbitrators appointed in accordance with the said rules of arbitration. All related proceedings should be at the place of the ICC in Paris, France.

The language to be used in the arbitral proceedings shall be English.

Note

The following letter from the Secretary General of ASD extends the special usage rights of this specification and has been included for information, without affecting the technical contents. The content of this letter will be included in the copyright information as part of the S-Series 2024 block release.

Special Usage Rights for the S-Series Specifications

To whom it may concern,

This letter seeks to clarify the special usage rights for the suite of documents known as the S-Series Specifications, for which the Aerospace and Defence Industries Association of Europe (ASD) holds the copyright and trademark.

The special usage rights are described as follows:

Permission to use or deliver training from the information contained in the S-Series Specifications, and the right to reproduce or publish the S-Series Specifications, in whole or in part, is hereby given to the following:

1. National Associations who are members of ASD and all their member companies;

2. Members of Aerospace Industries Association of America;

3. Members of the ATA e-Business Program;

4. Members of International Coordinating Council of Aerospace Industries Associations (ICCAIA) not included in categories 1 through 2 inclusively;

5. Airlines and Armed Forces that are customers of Companies included in Categories 1 through 3 inclusively;

6. Ministries of Defence of the member countries of ASD, of NATO and NATO Partners[1];

7. The Department of Defense of the USA;

8. NATO bodies, organizations & agencies;

9. Universities;

10. Technologies and Research Institutes.

Any further requirement for clarification, should in the first instance be directed to the Service Commission of the ASD.

Yours Sincerely,

Jan Pie

Secretary General of ASD

---

[1] as per: https://www.nato.int/cps/en/natohq/51288.htm);

Page intentionally blank.

End of data module

Table of contents

The listed documents are included in Issue 2.1, dated 2021-04-30, of this publication.

Chapter	Data module title	Data module code	Applic
Chap 3.6	Unit of functionality - Capability definition	SX002D-A-03-06-0000-00A-040A-A	All
Chap 3.7	Unit of functionality - Change information	SX002D-A-03-07-0000-00A-040A-A	All
Chap 3.8	Unit of functionality - Circuit breaker	SX002D-A-03-08-0000-00A-040A-A	All
Chap 3.9	Unit of functionality - Competence definition	SX002D-A-03-09-0000-00A-040A-A	All
Chap 3.10	Unit of functionality - Damage definition	SX002D-A-03-10-0000-00A-040A-A	All
Chap 3.11	Unit of functionality - Decision tree template definition	SX002D-A-03-11-0000-00A-040A-A	All
Chap 3.12	Unit of functionality - Design change request	SX002D-A-03-12-0000-00A-040A-A	All
Chap 3.13	Unit of functionality - Digital file	SX002D-A-03-13-0000-00A-040A-A	All
Chap 3.14	Unit of functionality - Document	SX002D-A-03-14-0000-00A-040A-A	All
Chap 3.15	Unit of functionality - Environment definition	SX002D-A-03-15-0000-00A-040A-A	All
Chap 3.16	Unit of functionality - Facility	SX002D-A-03-16-0000-00A-040A-A	All
Chap 3.17	Unit of functionality - Failure mode	SX002D-A-03-17-0000-00A-040A-A	All
Chap 3.18	Unit of functionality - Hardware element	SX002D-A-03-18-0000-00A-040A-A	All
Chap 3.19	Unit of functionality - In service optimization analysis	SX002D-A-03-19-0000-00A-040A-A	All
Chap 3.20	Unit of functionality - Location	SX002D-A-03-20-0000-00A-040A-A	All
Chap 3.21	Unit of functionality - Measurement point	SX002D-A-03-21-0000-00A-040A-A	All
Chap 3.22	Unit of functionality - Message	SX002D-A-03-22-0000-00A-040A-A	All
Chap 3.23	Unit of functionality - Mission definition	SX002D-A-03-23-0000-00A-040A-A	All
Chap 3.24	Unit of functionality - Organization	SX002D-A-03-24-0000-00A-040A-A	All
Chap 3.25	Unit of functionality - Part as realized	SX002D-A-03-25-0000-00A-040A-A	All
Chap 3.26	Unit of functionality - Part definition	SX002D-A-03-26-0000-00A-040A-A	All
Chap 3.27	Unit of functionality - Performance parameter	SX002D-A-03-27-0000-00A-040A-A	All
Chap 3.28	Unit of functionality - Product and project	SX002D-A-03-28-0000-00A-040A-A	All
Chap 3.29	Unit of functionality - Product design configuration	SX002D-A-03-29-0000-00A-040A-A	All
Chap 3.30	Unit of functionality - Product usage context	SX002D-A-03-30-0000-00A-040A-A	All

Chapter	Data module title	Data module code	Applic
Chap 3.31	Unit of functionality - Product usage phase	SX002D-A-03-31-0000-00A-040A-A	All
Chap 3.32	Unit of functionality - Remark	SX002D-A-03-32-0000-00A-040A-A	All
Chap 3.33	Unit of functionality - Resource specification	SX002D-A-03-33-0000-00A-040A-A	All
Chap 3.34	Unit of functionality - Security classification	SX002D-A-03-34-0000-00A-040A-A	All
Chap 3.35	Unit of functionality - Serialized part configuration	SX002D-A-03-35-0000-00A-040A-A	All
Chap 3.36	Unit of functionality - Serialized product variant configuration	SX002D-A-03-36-0000-00A-040A-A	All
Chap 3.37	Unit of functionality - Software element	SX002D-A-03-37-0000-00A-040A-A	All
Chap 3.38	Unit of functionality - Special event	SX002D-A-03-38-0000-00A-040A-A	All
Chap 3.39	Unit of functionality - Task	SX002D-A-03-39-0000-00A-040A-A	All
Chap 3.40	Unit of functionality - Task requirement	SX002D-A-03-40-0000-00A-040A-A	All
Chap 3.41	Unit of functionality - Task resource	SX002D-A-03-41-0000-00A-040A-A	All
Chap 3.42	Unit of functionality - Task usage	SX002D-A-03-42-0000-00A-040A-A	All
Chap 3.43	Unit of functionality - Time limit	SX002D-A-03-43-0000-00A-040A-A	All
Chap 3.44	Unit of functionality - Zone element	SX002D-A-03-44-0000-00A-040A-A	All

Applicable to: All

Page intentionally blank.

End of data module

Chapter 1

Introduction to the specification

Table of contents

SX002D-A-01-00-0000-00A-009A-A

Page intentionally blank.

Chapter 1.1

Purpose

Table of contents

List of tables

References

Table 1 References

Chap No./Document No.	Title
SX001G	Glossary for the S-Series ILS specifications
S1000D	International specification for technical publications using a common source database
SX000i	International guide for the use of the S-Series Integrated Logistics Support (ILS) specifications
UML	Unified Modeling Language (www.omg.org)

1   General

This chapter gives a basic overview of the SX002D purpose including the history of the development.

2   Purpose

The SX002D Common Data Model (CDM) for the S-Series Integrated Product Support (IPS) specifications is a conceptual description of all data elements common to two or more S-Series IPS specifications. Data defined as part of one S-Series IPS specification which are neither used by another specification nor matches any feedback data, can be excluded.

The purpose of SX002D is to harmonize data modeling activities that are performed within the respective S-Series IPS specification, and to consolidate data requirements into one coherent S-Series data model, using the Unified Modeling Language (UML). To support this, there is also a set of core object definitions which establishes the basic components that are used in the S-Series IPS specifications data models.

SX002D represents the harmonized end-state common terminology/model for all S-Series IPS specifications, not the current individual terminology/models used in the respective S-Series IPS

specification. The aim is to have the S-Series IPS specifications adopt the harmonized CDM terminology/model in future issues.

3 Background

The international aerospace and defense community has, over the past 25 years, invested considerable effort to develop specifications in the field of IPS. The work was accomplished by integrated working groups composed of industry and customer organizations in a collaborative environment. Working group participants included representatives from national ministries and departments of defense from Europe and the United States. Aerospace and defense associations provided guidance and supported the work as required. The structure and functional coverage of these specifications was largely determined by North Atlantic Treaty Organization (NATO) requirements specified during an international workshop in Paris in 1993.

Beginning in 2003, the relationships between supporting industry organizations were formalized through a series of Memorandums of Understanding (MOU). Initially AeroSpace and Defense Industries Association of Europe (ASD) and Aerospace Industries Association (AIA) signed an MOU to jointly develop and maintain S1000D, International specification for technical publications utilizing a common source database.

In 2010, ASD and AIA signed an MOU to promote a common, interoperable, international suite of Integrated Product Support (IPS) specifications and jointly develop the S-Series IPS specifications. This MOU authorized the formation of the ASD/AIA IPS Spec Council, whose responsibilities include performing liaison between ASD and AIA, developing and maintaining the S-Series IPS specifications, administering joint meetings and identifying additional areas of harmonization.

The need for a consolidated and harmonized data model was recognized as a fundamental requirement for the S-Series IPS specifications. The creation and maintenance of the common data model and its associated glossary (SX001G) was assigned to the Data Modeling and Exchange Working Group (DMEWG). As the common data model is a consolidation of concepts across the S-Series IPS specifications, the common data model is numbered SX002D to align it with SX000i, International guide for the use of the S-Series IPS specifications.

Chapter 1.2

Scope

Table of contents

Page

List of tables

References

Table 1 References

Chap No./Document No.	Title
S1000D	International specification for technical publications using a common source database
S1000X	Input data specification for S1000D
S1003X	S1000D to S3000L interchange specification
S2000M	International specification for materiel management - Integrated data processing
S2000X	Input data specification for S2000M
S3000L	International procedure specification for Logistics Support Analysis (LSA)
S3000X	Input data specification for S3000L
S4000P	International specification for developing and continuously improving preventive maintenance
S4000X	Input data specification for S4000P
S5000F	International specification for in-service data feedback
S6000T	International specification for training analysis and design
S6000X	Input data specification for S6000T
SX000i	International Guide for the Use of the S-Series Integrated Product Support (IPS) Specifications
SX001G	Glossary for the S-Series IPS specifications
SX004G	Unified Modeling Language (UML) model reader's guide
SX005G	S-Series ILS specification XML schema implementation guidance

1 General

SX002D is designed to harmonize data modeling activities performed within the respective S-Series IPS specification, and to consolidate data requirements into one coherent S-Series data model, using UML.

2 Scope

The scope of Issue 2.1 of SX002D is focused on areas needed to define and exchange information for a product, its breakdowns, allowed configurations, task definitions and serializations. The scope for previous issues of this specification was primarily derived from S1003X. This issue has also considered additional requirements identified in the more recent input data specifications. Definitions for all classes and attributes defined in the SX002D common data model are published as part of SX001G, and are therefore not repeated in this specification

The SX002D Common Data Model also includes published issues of S-Series Primitives and S-Series Compound Attributes.

3 Specifications

Multiple S-Series IPS specifications are currently available or in the process of development, including:

- S1000D   International specification for technical publications using a common source database
- S2000M   International specification for material management - Integrated data processing
- S3000L   International procedure specification for Logistics Support Analysis (LSA)
- S4000P   International specification for developing and continuously improving preventive maintenance
- S5000F   International specification for in-service data feedback
- S6000T   International specification for training analysis and design
- SX000i   International guide for the use of the S-Series Integrated Product Support (IPS) specifications
- SX001G   Glossary for the S-Series IPS specifications
- SX004G   Unified Modeling Language (UML) model reader's guide
- SX005G   S-Series ILS specification XML schema implementation guidance
- S1000X   Input data specification for S1000D
- S1003X   S1000D to S3000L interchange specification
- S2000X   Input data specification for S2000M
- S3000X   Input data specification for S3000L
- S4000X   Input data specification for S4000P
- S6000X   Input data specification for S6000T

Chapter 1.3

How to use the specification

Table of contents
Page

List of tables

References

Table 1 References

Chap No./Document No.	Title
SX004G	Unified Modeling Language (UML) model readers' guidance

1   General

This chapter gives an overview of the organization of the specification and the fundamental reading rules.

2   Acronyms

Acronyms are included to aid understanding and to minimize duplication. Acronyms used in SX002D are explained in this chapter. The same abbreviation is used for all tenses, the possessive case and singular and plural forms of a given word.

Acronyms used in SX002D are:

- AIA   Aerospace Industries Association of America
- ASD   AeroSpace and Defence Industries Association of Europe
- CDM   Common Data Model
- DMEWG Data Modeling and Exchange Working Group
- ILS   Integrated Logistics Support
- ISO   International Organization for Standardization
- LSA   Logistics Support Analysis
- MOU   Memorandum of Understanding
- MSG   Maintenance Steering Group
- NATO   North Atlantic Treaty Organization

- NCAGE   NATO Commercial and Governmental Entity
- OASIS   Organization for the Advancement of Structured Information Standards
- PLCS   Product Life Cycle Support
- UML   Unified Modeling Language
- UoF   Unit of Functionality

3 Organization of the specification

3.1 Chapter 1 - Introduction to the specification

Chap 1 provides a summarized view on purpose, background, scope and maintenance of SX002D.

3.2 Chapter 2 - Core object definitions

Chap 2 defines the S-Series primitives and compound attributes which must be used as the basic data types throughout all data models defined for the respective S-Series IPS specifications including the Common Data Model (CDM).

Chap 2 also defines the core characteristics which are implemented by all Classes defined in the CDM, including the capability to define project specific attributes.

All S-Series primitives, compound attributes and core object definitions, are defined using Unified Modeling Language (UML) class models. More information on how to read the UML class models is described in SX004G.

3.3 Chapter 3 – Units of functionality

Chap 3 defines the business-oriented data model using UML class models. Chap 3 is subdivided into a set of business-oriented Unit of Functionalities (UoF).

The respective UoF in Chap 3 are defined in alphabetical order for easy referencing from other S-Series IPS specifications. The respective S-Series IPS specification that builds on the CDM may present its UoFs in a different order based on business process.

For readers who are interested in the CDM as a stand-alone data model, the suggested order of reading the UoFs is:

- Overall Product, Project and support context information

  - Chap 3.28   Unit of functionality - Product and project
  - Chap 3.30   Unit of functionality - Product usage context
  - Chap 3.23   Unit of functionality - Mission definition
  - Chap 3.31   Unit of functionality - Product usage phase
  - Chap 3.6   Unit of functionality - Capability definition
  - Chap 3.15   Unit of functionality - Environment definition
  - Chap 3.27   Unit of functionality - Performance parameter
  - Chap 3.16   Unit of functionality - Facility
  - Chap 3.20   Unit of functionality - Location

- Definition of the Product including its systems, functions, zones, parts etc

  - Chap 3.5   Unit of functionality - Breakdown structure
  - Chap 3.26   Unit of functionality - Part definition
  - Chap 3.18   Unit of functionality - Hardware element
  - Chap 3.37   Unit of functionality - Software element
  - Chap 3.2   Unit of functionality - Aggregated element
  - Chap 3.44   Unit of functionality - Zone element
  - Chap 3.29   Unit of functionality - Product design configuration

- Definition of analysis candidates and support analysis activities

- [Chap 3.3](#)   Unit of functionality - Analysis candidate item
- [Chap 3.17](#)   Unit of functionality - Failure mode
- [Chap 3.38](#)   Unit of functionality - Special event
- [Chap 3.10](#)   Unit of functionality - Damage definition
- [Chap 3.11](#)   Unit of functionality - Decision tree template definition
- [Chap 3.19](#)   Unit of functionality - In service optimization analysis

– Definition of support tasks defined for the Product and its constituent parts

- [Chap 3.40](#)   Unit of functionality - Task requirement
- [Chap 3.12](#)   Unit of functionality - Design change request
- [Chap 3.39](#)   Unit of functionality - Task
- [Chap 3.8](#)   Unit of functionality - Circuit breaker
- [Chap 3.41](#)   Unit of functionality - Task resource
- [Chap 3.9](#)   Unit of functionality - Competence definition
- [Chap 3.33](#)   Unit of functionality - Resource specification
- [Chap 3.42](#)   Unit of functionality - Task usage
- [Chap 3.43](#)   Unit of functionality - Time limit

– Definition of serialized Product and Part individuals

- [Chap 3.25](#)   Unit of functionality - Part as realized
- [Chap 3.35](#)   Unit of functionality - Serialized part configuration
- [Chap 3.36](#)   Unit of functionality - Serialized product variant configuration
- [Chap 3.21](#)   Unit of functionality - Measurement point

– Generic capabilities which can be used to assign additional associated information with each core business object

- [Chap 3.7](#)   Unit of functionality - Change information
- [Chap 3.14](#)   Unit of functionality - Document
- [Chap 3.13](#)   Unit of functionality - Digital file
- [Chap 3.24](#)   Unit of functionality - Organization
- [Chap 3.34](#)   Unit of functionality - Security classification
- [Chap 3.32](#)   Unit of functionality - Remark
- [Chap 3.4](#)   Unit of functionality - Applicability statement

– Definition of messages and message content

- [Chap 3.22](#)   Unit of functionality - Message

SX002D-A-01-03-0000-00A-040A-A

Page intentionally blank.

Chapter 1.4

Maintenance of the specification

Table of contents

Page

List of tables

References

Table 1 References

Chap No./Document No.	Title
SX000i	International guide for the use of the S-Series Integrated Logistics Support (ILS) specifications
IPS-C-2020-010	Governance of the S-Series IPS specifications

1   Maintenance of the specification

SX002D is maintained by the Data Modeling and Exchange Working Group (DMEWG) operating under the supervision of the Integrated Product Support (IPS) Specifications Council. Both the DMEWG and the IPS Specifications Council include representatives from AeroSpace and Defense Industries Association of Europe (ASD) and Aerospace Industries Association (AIA) member companies and nations.

Issues related to SX002D can be raised using the change request tool found at www.SX000i.org/CPF/login_page.php. Change requests are submitted with the understanding that any revisions to SX002D can affect the other specifications in the S-Series IPS specifications, and that proposed changes are subject to international agreement between ASD and AIA member companies and nations.

Upon receipt of a change request, the DMEWG will follow the change management process described in IPS-C-2020-010, to gain consensus agreement from the participating organizations prior to the publication of changes. The DMEWG considers change proposals and ratifies them for incorporation into SX002D.

Page intentionally blank.

Applicable to: All

End of data module

DMC-SX002D-A-01-04-0000-00A-040A-A_004-00_EN-US

Chapter 2

Core object definitions

Table of contents

Page intentionally blank.

Applicable to: All

End of data module

DMC-SX002D-A-02-00-0000-00A-009A-A_004-00_EN-US

Chapter 2.1

Core object definitions - S-Series primitives

Table of contents

Page

List of tables

References

Table 1 References

Chap No./Document No.	Title
None	

1   Description

S-Series primitives represent data types which are used to determine the type of values that individual attributes in the S-Series IPS specifications data models can have.

S-Series primitives used in the S-Series IPS specifications are different from those data types typically used in other data models, eg, integer, real, and string. In order to create a richer data model, a set of more complex data types has been defined. The primary purpose for these S-Series primitives is to allow for further characterizations of attribute values in order to record valuable metadata for each value. These characterizations are defined to support eg, recording multiple values over time, keeping values in different languages, etc. Also, applicability statements are part of the additional characterization that can be associated with single attribute values.

The S-Series IPS specifications data models also enable simple data types through S-Series UML primitives. The rationale for defining explicit UML `<<primitive>>` classes for existing UML primitives is to also allow for additional characterizations to be assigned to these data types eg, applicability statements.

Page intentionally blank.

Chapter 2.1.1

S-Series primitives - ClassificationType

Table of contents

Page

List of tables

List of figures

References

Table 1 References

Chap No./Document No.	Title
None	

1   Description

`ClassificationType` is an S-Series IPS specification's defined `<<primitive>>` that represents a finite set of values which are used to characterize the associated information for a defined purpose. Refer to Fig 1.

2   UML class model

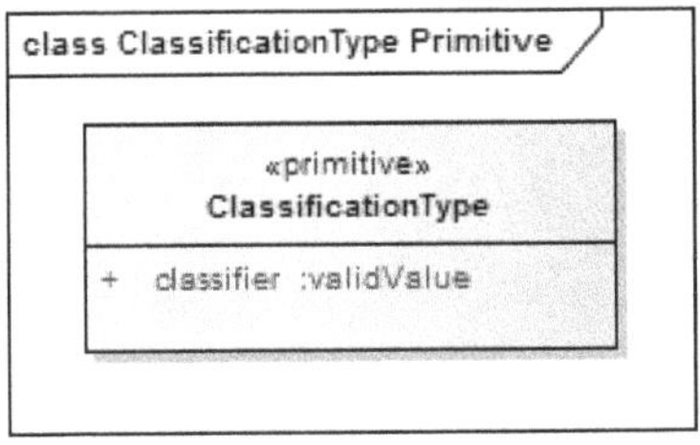

ICN-B6865-SX002D0013-002-01

Fig 1 S-Series primitive classification type - UML class model

Applicable to: All

Page intentionally blank.

Chapter 2.1.2

S-Series primitives - DateTimeType

Table of contents

List of tables

List of figures

References

Table 1 References

Chap No./Document No.	Title
None	

1   Description

Date and time-oriented primitives support the representation of Gregorian calendar dates with an optional extension where also time, down to seconds, on a particular day can be represented using the 24-hour time scale.

`DateType` is an S-Series IPS specification's defined `<<primitive>>` that represent Gregorian calendar dates. Refer to Fig 1.

`DateTimeType` is an S-Series IPS specification's defined `<<primitive>>` that extends the `DateType` `<<primitive>>` with the capability to also represent time on a particular day together with an optional oriented offset from Coordinated Universal Time. Refer to Fig 1.

2 UML class model

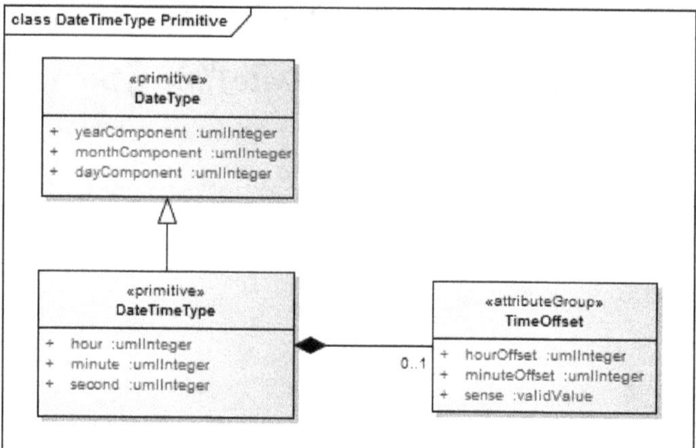

ICN-B6865-SX002D0014-002-01

Fig 1 S-Series primitive DateTimeType - UML class model

Chapter 2.1.3

S-Series primitives - DescriptorType

Table of contents
Page

List of tables

List of figures

References

Table 1 References

Chap No./Document No.	Title
None	

1   Description

`DescriptorType` is an S-Series IPS specification's defined `<<primitive>>` that represents any form of textual data (free form) along with its core characterizations. Refer to Fig 2.

Note

Core characterizations for the `DescriptorType` `descriptorText` attribute include:

- `descriptorLanguage`, that determines the language in which the `descriptorText` is written
- `descriptorProvidedBy`, which identifies the organization that provided the `descriptorText`
- `descriptorProvidedDate`, which defines when the `descriptorText` was provided

2 UML class model

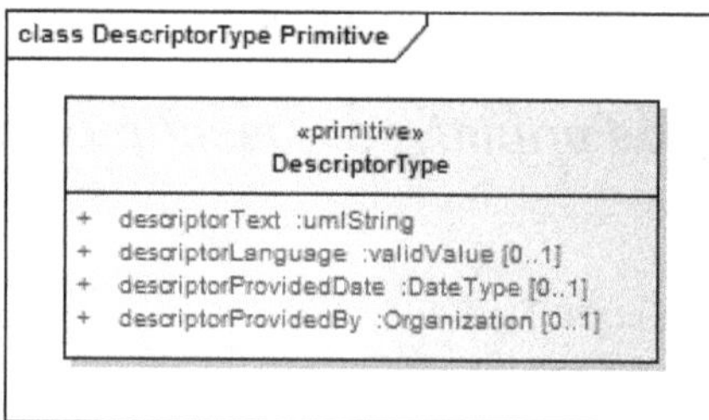

ICN-B6865-SX002D0015-002-01

Fig 1 S-Series primitive DescriptorType - UML class model

Chapter 2.1.4

S-Series primitives - IdentifierType

Table of contents

Page

List of tables

List of figures

References

Table 1 References

Chap No./Document No.	Title
None	

1   Description

`IdentifierType` is an S-Series IPS specification's defined `<<primitive>>` that represents any kind of identification along with its core characterizations. Refer to Fig 2.

Note

Core characterizations for the `IdentifierType` `identifier` attribute include:

- `identifierClassifier`, which determines the meaning of the `identifier`
- `identifierSetBy`, which identifies the organization that is responsible for the `identifier`

2 UML class model

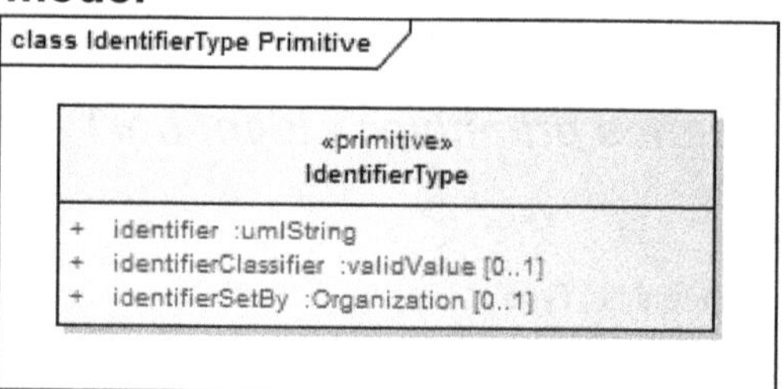

ICN-B6865-SX002D0016-002-01

Fig 1 S-Series primitive IdentifierType - UML class model

Chapter 2.1.5

S-Series primitives - NameType

Table of contents
Page

List of tables

List of figures

References

Table 1 References

Chap No./Document No.	Title
None	

1   Description

`NameType` is an S-Series IPS specification's defined `<<primitive>>` that represents an informal identification. Refer to Fig 2.

Note

Core characterizations for the `NameType nameText` attribute include:

- `nameLanguage`, that determines the language in which the `nameText` is written
- `nameProvidedBy`, which identifies the `Organization` that defined the `nameText`

2   UML class model

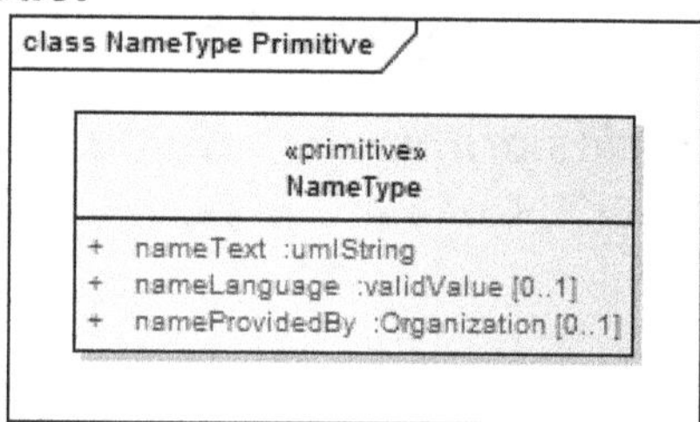

ICN-B6865-SX002D0023-001-01

Fig 1 S-Series primitive NameType - UML class model

Chapter 2.1.6

S-Series primitives - PropertyType

Table of contents

List of tables

List of figures

References

Table 1 References

Chap No./Document No.	Title
None	

1   Description

`PropertyType` primitives support the representation of a measurable characteristic along with its core characterizations.

The `PropertyType` `<<primitive>>` has a set of specializations which can be used to represent an individual measurable characteristic, either using numeric value(s) with unit or a text value.

Note

Text values are typically used to represent values such as "AsRequired".

There are four different specializations of `PropertyType`, which can be used to represent an individual property value (Refer to Fig 1). These are:

-   `SingleValuePropertyType`, which is a `NumericalPropertyType` that specifies a single `value` and its `unit`
-   `ValueWithTolerancesPropertyType`, which is a `NumericalPropertyType` that specifies a range of values by specifying a single `nominalValue` and its `unit` together with the permitted variations from the nominal value
-   `ValueRangePropertyType`, which is a `NumericalPropertyType` that specifies a value pair that represents the range limits and their `unit`

   –   `TextPropertyType`, which is a `PropertyType` that specifies the value in text format

Note

Core characterizations for the `PropertyType` value(s) attribute(s) include:

- `valueDetermination`, that qualifies the method by which the value of the property has been determined
- `valueRecordingDateTime`, which identifies the calendar date and time when the property value was established

2   UML class model

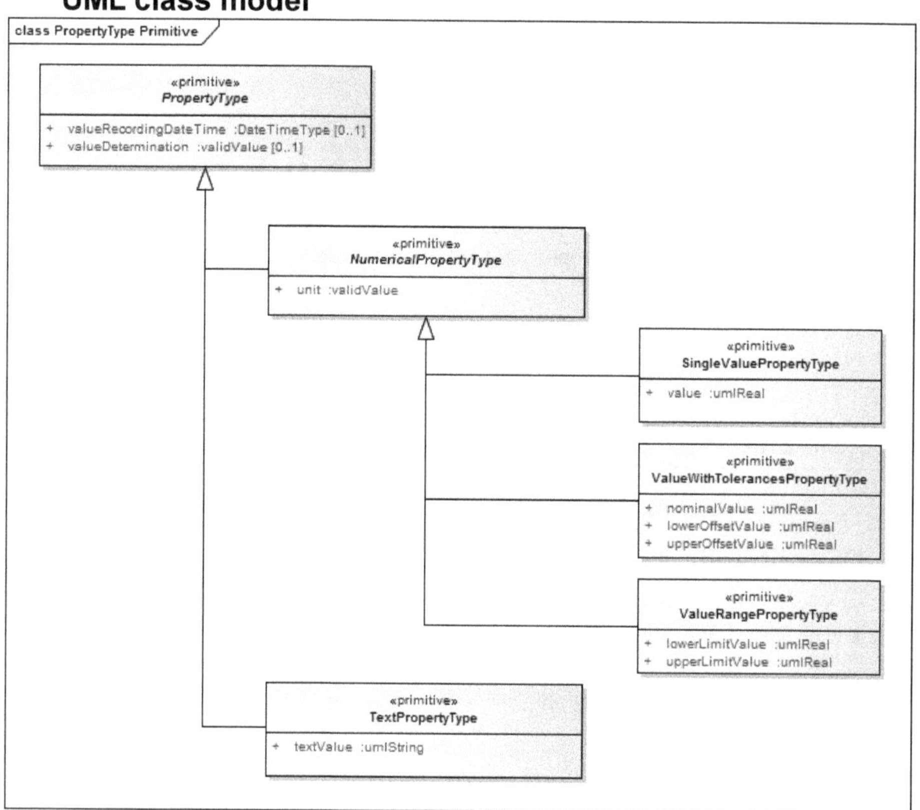

ICN-B6865-SX002D0017-002-01

Fig 1 S-Series primitive PropertyType - UML class model

Chapter 2.1.7

S-Series primitives - StateType

Table of contents

Page

List of tables

List of figures

References

Table 1 References

Chap No./Document No.	Title
None	

1   Description

`StateType` is an S-Series IPS specification's defined `<<primitive>>` that represents a particular condition that something is in at a particular time. Refer to Fig 1.

Note

Core characterizations for the `StateType` `state` attribute include:

- `stateRecordingDateTime`, which identifies the calendar date and time when the `state` was established

2   UML class model

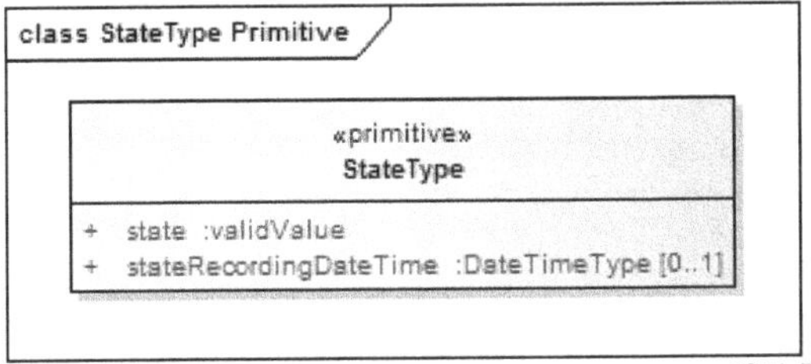

ICN-B6865-SX002D0024-001-01

Fig 1 S-Series primitive StateType - UML class model

Page intentionally blank.

Chapter 2.1.8

S-Series primitives - UML primitives

Table of contents

List of tables

List of figures

References

Table 1 References

Chap No./Document No.	Title
None	

1 Description

UML primitives are S-Series IPS specification's UML representations of core UML primitives. The rationale for defining S-Series IPS specifications specific <<umlPrimitive>> representations for the respective UML primitive, is to enable additional characterizations to be applied to each individual UML primitive, and to enable its use in project specific attributes (Refer to Chap 2.3). For the UML class diagram refer to Fig 1.

The following UML primitives have a corresponding <<umlPrimitive>>:

- Boolean
- Integer
- String
- Real
- Unlimited natural

2 UML class model

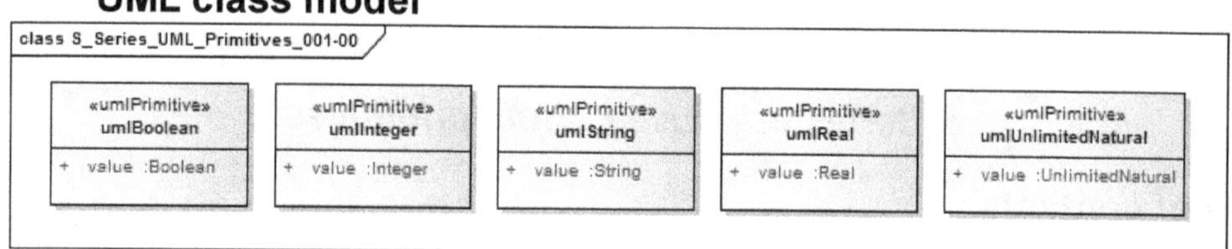

Fig 1   S-Series UML primitives - UML class model

Chapter 2.2

Core object definitions - S-Series compound attributes

Table of contents

List of tables

List of figures

References

Table 1 References

Chap No./Document No.	Title
None	

1   Description

A compound attribute is a combination of attributes, which establishes a pattern that can be reused in different contexts. Refer to Fig 1.

There are currently ten defined S-Series IPS specification's compound attributes:

- `AuthorizedLife`, represents the maximum usage limit and upon reaching this limit any further usage of the item must be re-authorized
- `DatedClassification`, represents a classification in conjunction with its recording date
- `DateRange`, specifies an interval of dates
- `DateTimeRange`, specifies an interval of date and times
- `SerialNumberRange`, specifies an interval of serialized items
- `ThreeDimensional`, represents spatial magnitudes. There are three defined specialization of the `ThreeDimensional` `<<compoundAttribute>>`:

  - `Cylinder`, represents a three-dimensional object with straight parallel sides and a circular section
  - `Cuboid`, represents a three-dimensional object where all its faces are rectangles and all angles are right angles
  - `Sphere`, represents a three-dimensional object where every point on its surface is equidistant from its center

- `TimeStampedClassification`, represents a classification in conjunction with its recording time stamp

2 UML class model

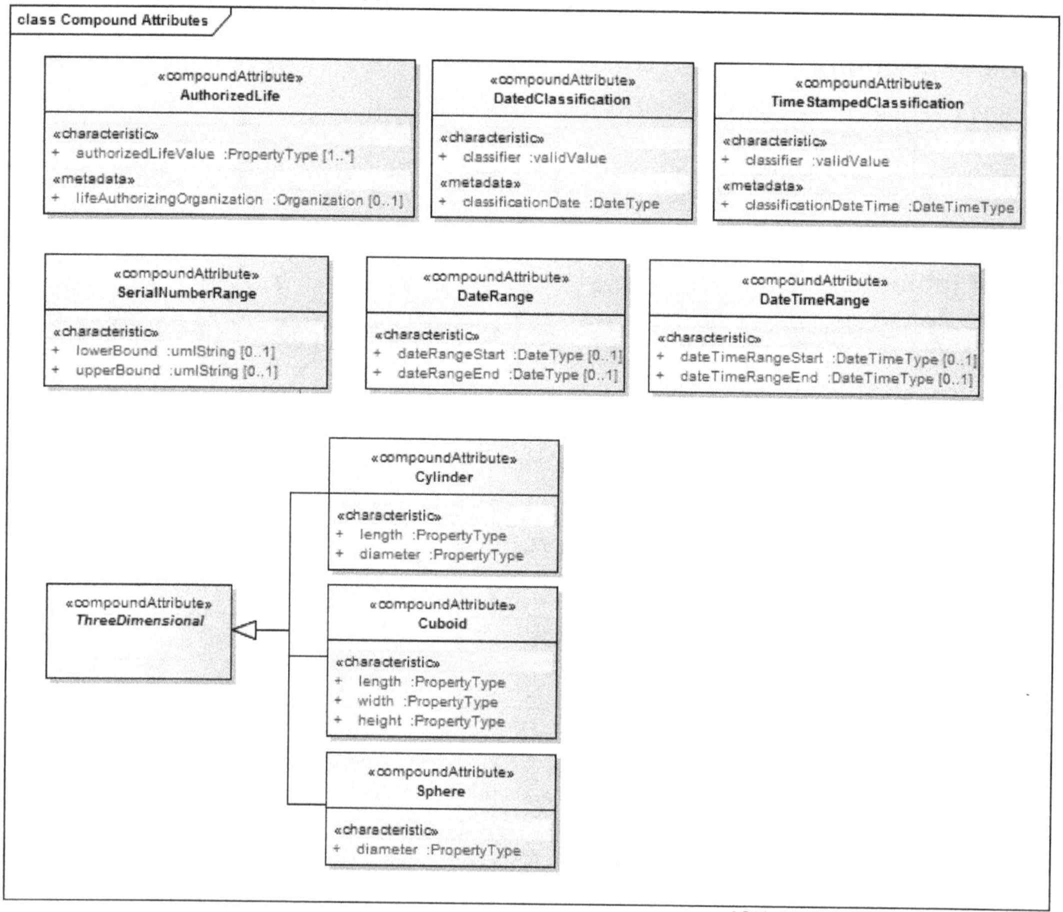

Fig 1 S-Series compound attributes - UML class model

ICN-B6865-SX002D0026-002-01

Chapter 2.3

Core object definitions - S-Series base object definition

Table of contents

Page

List of tables

List of figures

References

Table 1 References

Chap No./Document No.	Title
None	

1 Description

The `BaseObject` definition represents the core information inherent to any UML class and provides the capability to extend it with project specific attributes. Refer to Fig 1.

Note:
 Core characterizations of any UML class include:

- `uid`, which provides the capability to uniquely identify an instance of an UML class in the context of a specific exchange file (XML document)
- `uri`, which provides the capability to uniquely identify an instance of an UML class in the context of the World Wide Web
- `crud`, which identifies the change operation to a class instance represented in the exchange file. A change is always relative to the latest exchanged values for the class instance. Change operations include create, read (retrieve), update and delete

Project specific attributes provide the capability to extend any class with characteristics that are peculiar to a specific implementation.

Note
 The definition and scope for a project specific attribute must be defined in a separate XML schema as part of the exchange definition.

2   UML class model

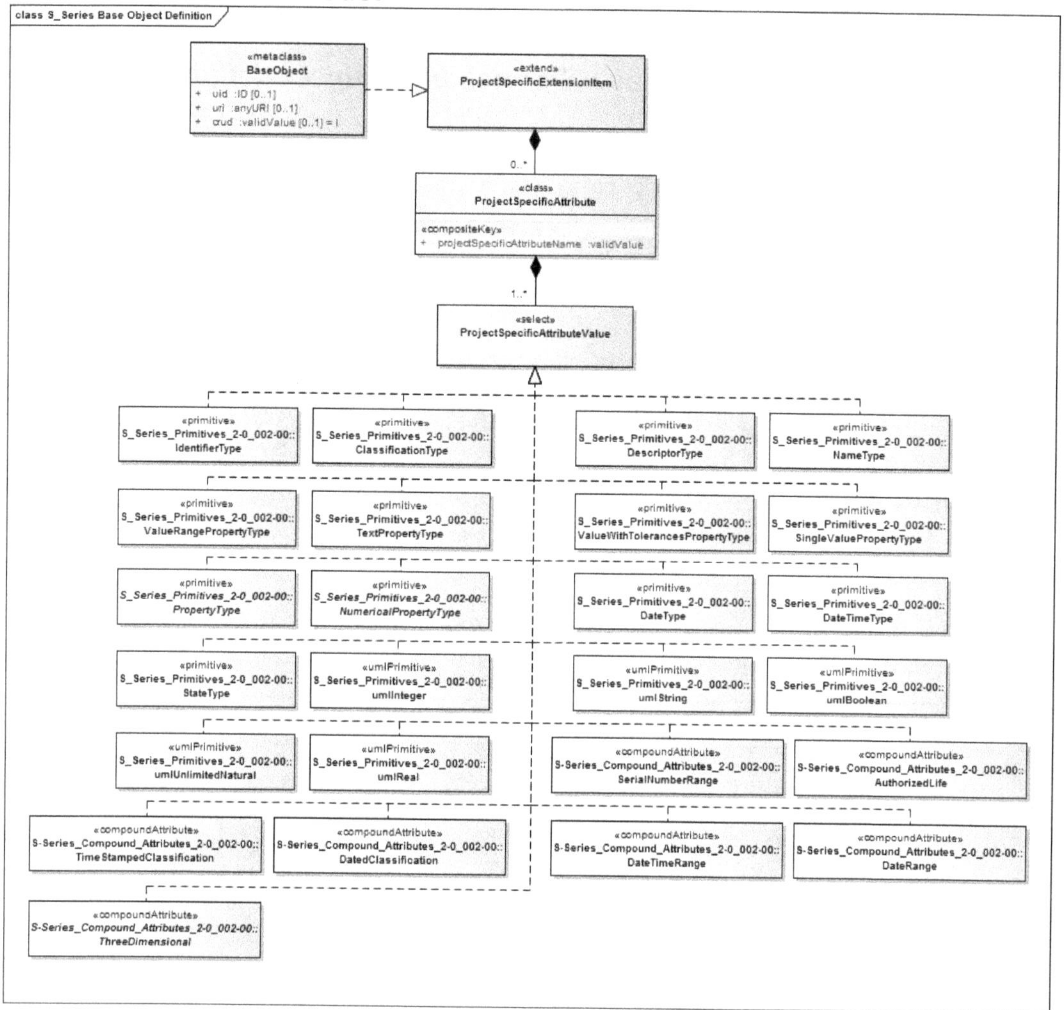

class S_Series Base Object Definition

«metaclass»
BaseObject
+ uid :ID [0..1]
+ uri :anyURI [0..1]
+ crud :validValue [0..1] = I

«extend»
ProjectSpecificExtensionItem

0..*

«class»
ProjectSpecificAttribute
«compositeKey»
+ projectSpecificAttributeName :validValue

1..*

«select»
ProjectSpecificAttributeValue

«primitive»
S_Series_Primitives_2-0_002-00::
IdentifierType

«primitive»
S_Series_Primitives_2-0_002-00::
ClassificationType

«primitive»
S_Series_Primitives_2-0_002-00::
DescriptorType

«primitive»
S_Series_Primitives_2-0_002-00::
NameType

«primitive»
S_Series_Primitives_2-0_002-00::
ValueRangePropertyType

«primitive»
S_Series_Primitives_2-0_002-00::
TextPropertyType

«primitive»
S_Series_Primitives_2-0_002-00::
ValueWithTolerancesPropertyType

«primitive»
S_Series_Primitives_2-0_002-00::
SingleValuePropertyType

«primitive»
S_Series_Primitives_2-0_002-00::
PropertyType

«primitive»
S_Series_Primitives_2-0_002-00::
NumericalPropertyType

«primitive»
S_Series_Primitives_2-0_002-00::
DateType

«primitive»
S_Series_Primitives_2-0_002-00::
DateTimeType

«primitive»
S_Series_Primitives_2-0_002-00::
StateType

«umlPrimitive»
S_Series_Primitives_2-0_002-00::
umlInteger

«umlPrimitive»
S_Series_Primitives_2-0_002-00::
umlString

«umlPrimitive»
S_Series_Primitives_2-0_002-00::
umlBoolean

«umlPrimitive»
S_Series_Primitives_2-0_002-00::
umlUnlimitedNatural

«umlPrimitive»
S_Series_Primitives_2-0_002-00::
umlReal

«compoundAttribute»
S-Series_Compound_Attributes_2-0_002-00::
SerialNumberRange

«compoundAttribute»
S-Series_Compound_Attributes_2-0_002-00::
AuthorizedLife

«compoundAttribute»
S-Series_Compound_Attributes_2-0_002-00::
TimeStampedClassification

«compoundAttribute»
S-Series_Compound_Attributes_2-0_002-00::
DatedClassification

«compoundAttribute»
S-Series_Compound_Attributes_2-0_002-00::
DateTimeRange

«compoundAttribute»
S-Series_Compound_Attributes_2-0_002-00::
DateRange

«compoundAttribute»
S-Series_Compound_Attributes_2-0_002-00::
ThreeDimensional

ICN-B6865-SX002D0027-004-01

Fig 1   S- Series base object definition - UML class model

Applicable to: All

End of data module

Chapter 3

Units of functionality

Table of contents

Chapter 3.1

Unit of functionality - Introduction

Table of contents

List of tables

References

Table 1 References

Chap No./Document No.	Title
None	

1   Introduction

The Common Data Model (CDM) is organized into a set of Units of Functionalities (UoF). Each UoF defines a set of data elements that together support the definition of data for a particular subject.

A UoF may refer to data elements in other UoFs to bring the referred data into larger contexts.

Splitting the CDM into a set of UoFs provides small and coherent portions of the data model to help the reader understand the complete data model.

Page intentionally blank.

Chapter 3.2

Unit of functionality - Aggregated element

Table of contents
Page

List of tables

List of figures

References

Table 1 References

Chap No./Document No.	Title
Chap 3.5	Unit of functionality - Breakdown structure

1   Description

The aggregated element UoF provides the capability to specify that an element within a breakdown represents a collection of elements for an identified purpose.

Example:

Examples of `AggregatedElement` are system, function and family.

Key features of the UoF aggregated element data model (Refer to Fig 1) are:

- `AggregatedElement` is a specialization of `BreakdownElement` (refer to Chap 3.5), which means that wherever `BreakdownElement` is being used in the data model, `AggregatedElement` can be used instead
- `AggregatedElementRevision` is a specialization of `BreakdownElementRevision` (refer to Chap 3.5), which means that wherever `BreakdownElementRevision` is being used in the data model, `AggregatedElementRevision` can be used instead

2 UML class model

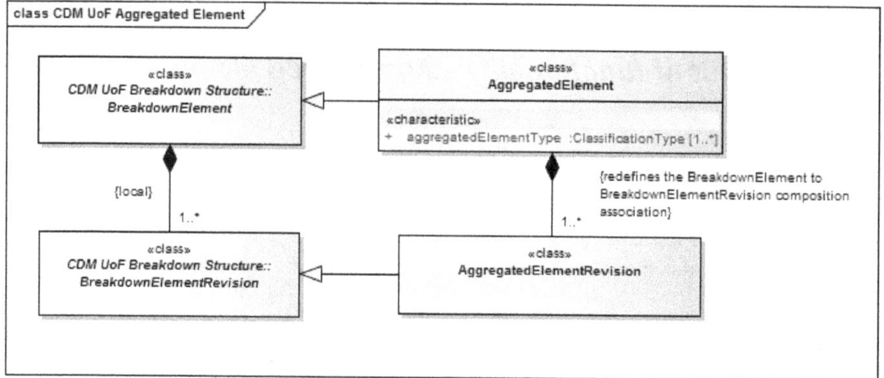

ICN-B6865-SX002D0004-004-01

Fig 1 UoF Aggregated element - UML class model

Chapter 3.3

Unit of functionality - Analysis candidate item

Table of contents

Page

List of tables

List of figures

References

Table 1 References

Chap No./Document No.	Title
Chap 3.5	Unit of functionality - Breakdown structure
Chap 3.26	Unit of functionality - Part definition
Chap 3.28	Unit of functionality - Product and project

1   Description

The analysis candidate item UoF provides the capability to define decisions and results associated with support analysis activities.

Key features of the UoF analysis candidate item data model (Refer to Fig 1) are:

- An `AnalysisCandidateItem` can be associated with zero, one or many `AnalysisActivity`'s where the `analysisActivityType` attribute determines the type of `AnalysisActivity` that has been considered, and possibly also carried out depending on the `analysisActivityDecision`
- An `AnalysisActivity` can be performed for the entire `Product` (refer to Chap 3.28), for a given `ProductVariant`, or for a portion thereof eg, a `BreakdownElement` (refer to Chap 3.5) or a `PartAsDesigned` (refer to Chap 3.26)

2   UML class model

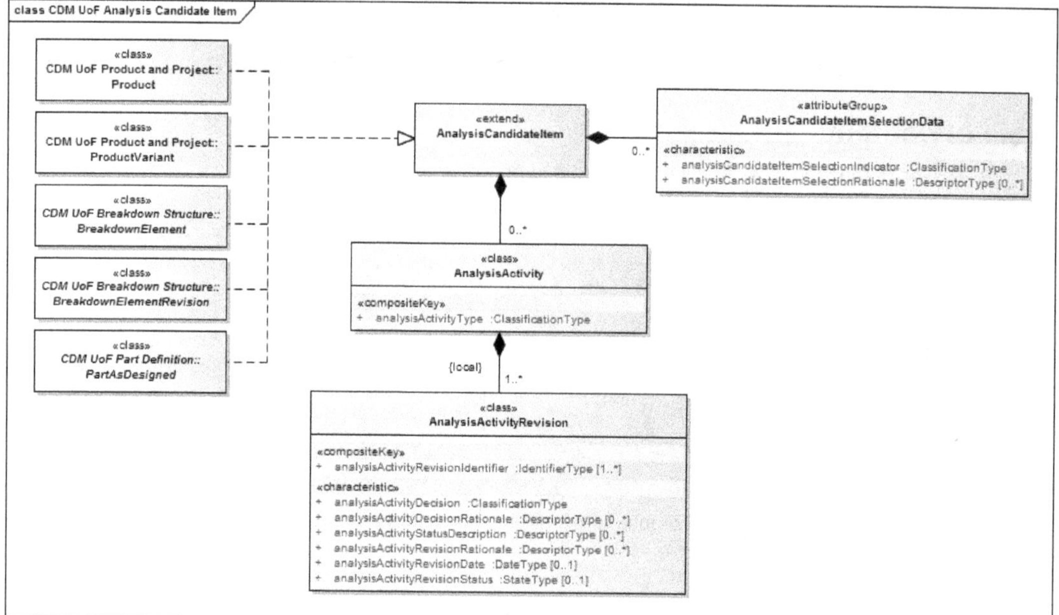

ICN-B6865-SX002D0046-001-01

Fig 1 UoF Analysis candidate item - UML class model

Chapter 3.4

Unit of functionality - Applicability statement

Table of contents

List of tables

List of figures

References

Table 1 References

Chap No./Document No.	Title
None	

1 Description

The applicability statement UoF provides the capability to define the situation or situations under which related items are valid.

Key features of the UoF applicability statement data model (Refer to Fig 1) are:

- It consists of three major components:

  - the identification and definition of the applicability statement
  - the definition of the evaluation expression (`EvaluationCriteria`)
  - the identification of the data that is to be asserted

- `ApplicabilityStatement` does not require an `EvaluationCriteria` but can contain only a textual expression
- `EvaluationCriteria` is always computer interpretable ie, it can be calculated to be 'TRUE' or 'FALSE'
- `EvaluationCriteria` must be defined as either:
  - `LogicalAND`
  - `LogicalOR`
  - `LogicalXOR`
  - `LogicalNOT`

- • `EvaluationByNestedApplicabilityStatement`
  - • `EvaluationByAssertionOfClassInstance`
  - • `EvaluationByAssertionOfSerializedItems`
  - • `EvaluationByAssertionOfCondition`

- The value to be asserted can either be an existing value defined by other classes in the data model (`EvaluationByAssertionOfClassInstance` or `EvaluationByAssertionOfSerializedItems`) or be an additional condition defined by a `ConditionType` along with a set of values (`ConditionTypeAssertMember`)

2 UML class model

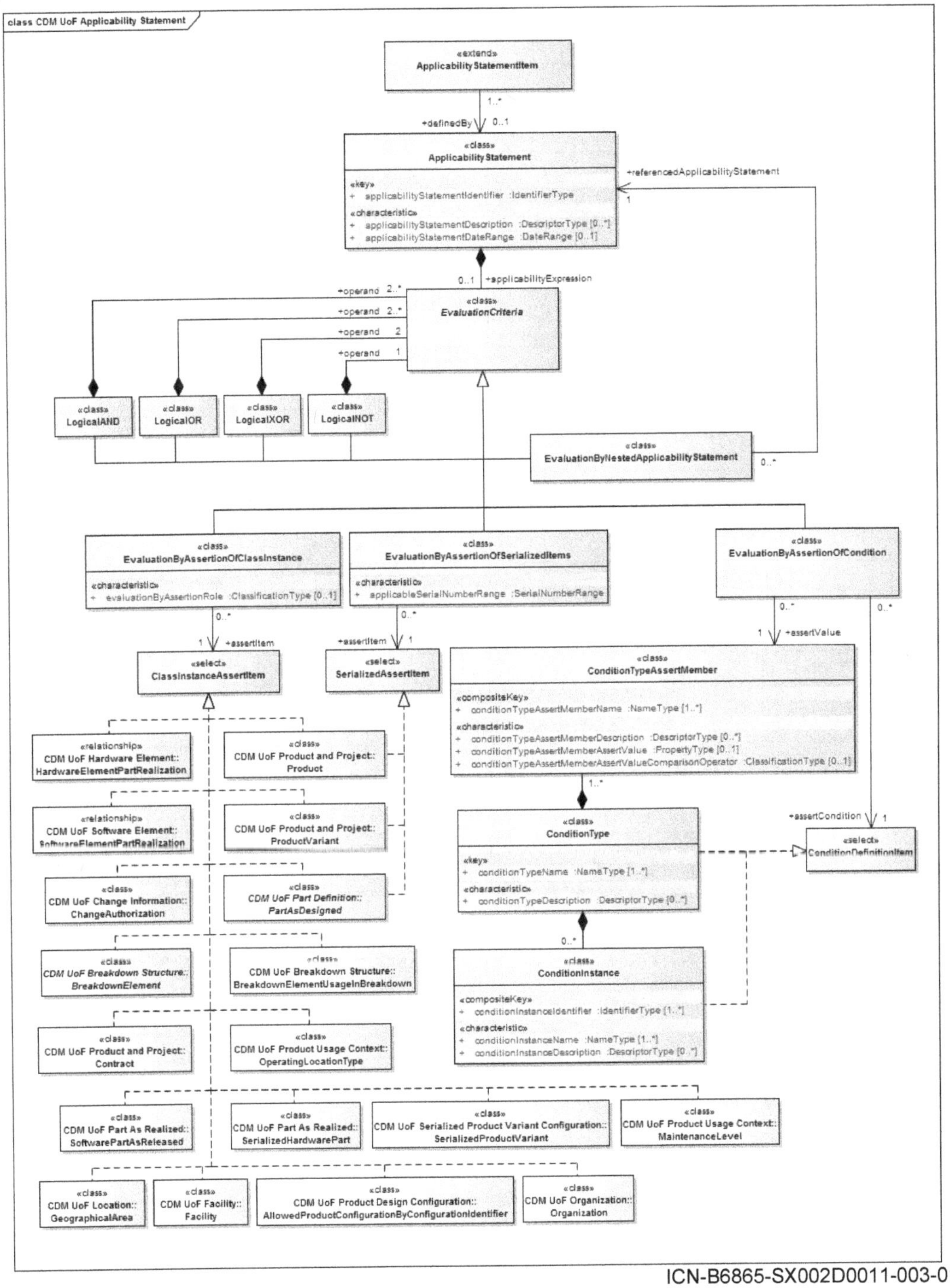

ICN-B6865-SX002D0011-003-01

Fig 1 UoF Applicability statement - UML class model

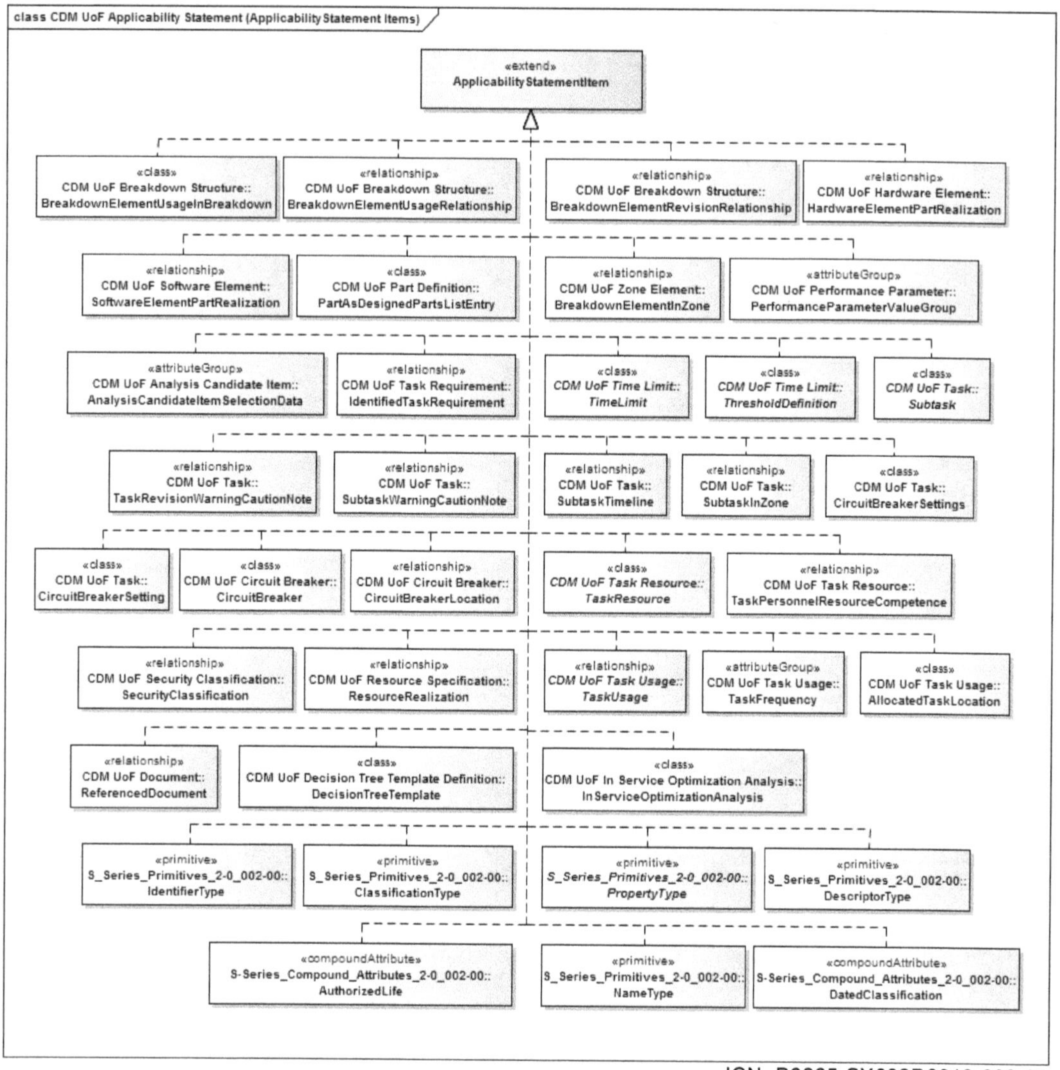

class CDM UoF Applicability Statement (Applicability Statement Items)

ICN -B6865-SX002D0019-003-01

Fig 2 UoF Applicability statement - Applicability statement items - UML class model

Chapter 3.5

Unit of functionality - Breakdown structure

Table of contents

Page

List of tables

List of figures

References

Table 1 References

Chap No./Document No.	Title
Chap 3.28	Unit of functionality - Product and project

1   Description

The breakdown structure UoF provides the capability to define one or many types of breakdowns for a specific `Product` or `ProductVariant` (refer to Chap 3.28).

Examples

Examples of breakdown types are functional, physical, system, zonal or hybrid. A hybrid breakdown structure is a combination of different types of breakdown elements.

Key features of the UoF breakdown structure data model (Refer to Fig 1) are:

- `Breakdown`'s can be defined either for the overall `Product` (including its `ProductVariants`) or for a specific `ProductVariant`
- Each `Breakdown` can have one or many `BreakdownRevisions`, where each `BreakdownRevision` references the `BreakdownElementRevisions` that are included in the specific revision of the `Breakdown`
- References between a `BreakdownRevision` and its constituent `BreakdownElement`'s are established using the `BreakdownElementUsageInBreakdown` class
- `BreakdownElements` included in a `BreakdownRevision` can be organized hierarchically into a breakdown structure by applying the `BreakdownElementStructure` construct to instances of `BreakdownElementUsageInBreakdown`.

Note

There must be one instance of `BreakdownElementUsageInBreakdown` that has no parent element. This instance of `BreakdownElementUsageInBreakdown` is often referred to as the root node.

The breakdown structure UoF allows for a defined `BreakdownElement` and its revisions to be part of many `Breakdown`'s and/or revisions thereof. A `BreakdownElement` (revision) can be positioned differently in the respective `Breakdown` and/or revision thereof.

Note

Each instance of `BreakdownElementUsageInBreakdown` and `BreakdownElementStructure` is uniquely defined in the context of a specific `BreakdownRevision`.

2   UML class model

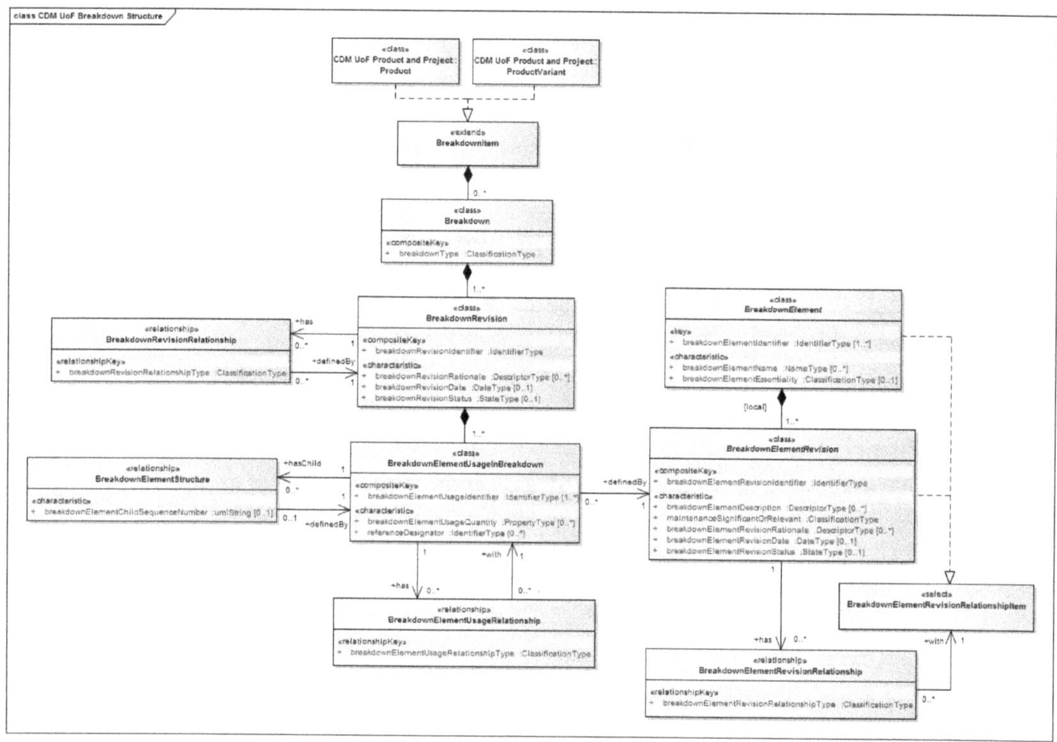

ICN-B6865-SX002D0002-003-01

Fig 1 UoF breakdown structure - UML class model

Chapter 3.6

Unit of functionality - Capability definition

Table of contents

List of tables

List of figures

References

Table 1 References

Chap No./Document No.	Title
None	

1   Description

The capability definition UoF provides the possibility to define functional and physical abilities enabled by the associated item.

Example:

> Examples of `CapabilityDefinition` are air-to-air refuel, deep water exploration, and body detection.

Key features of the UoF capability definition data model (Refer to Fig 1) are:

- Each associated `CapabilityDefinitionItem` can have zero, one or many defined capabilities
- Each `CapabilityDefinition` can have zero, one or many documented characteristics

2   UML class model

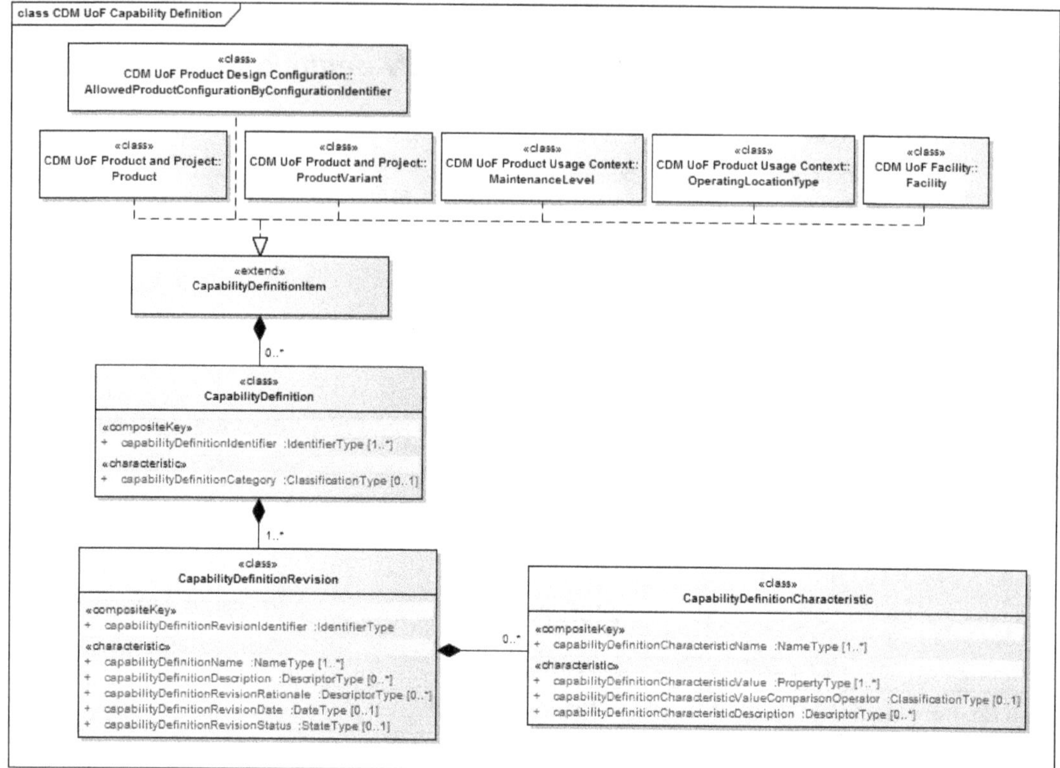

ICN-B6865-SX002D0047-001-01

Fig 1 UoF Capability definition - UML class model

Chapter 3.7

Unit of functionality - Change information

Table of contents

List of tables

List of figures

References

Table 1 References

Chap No./Document No.	Title
None	

1   Description

The change information UoF provides the capability to identify that an item has been affected by an authorized change.

2 UML class model

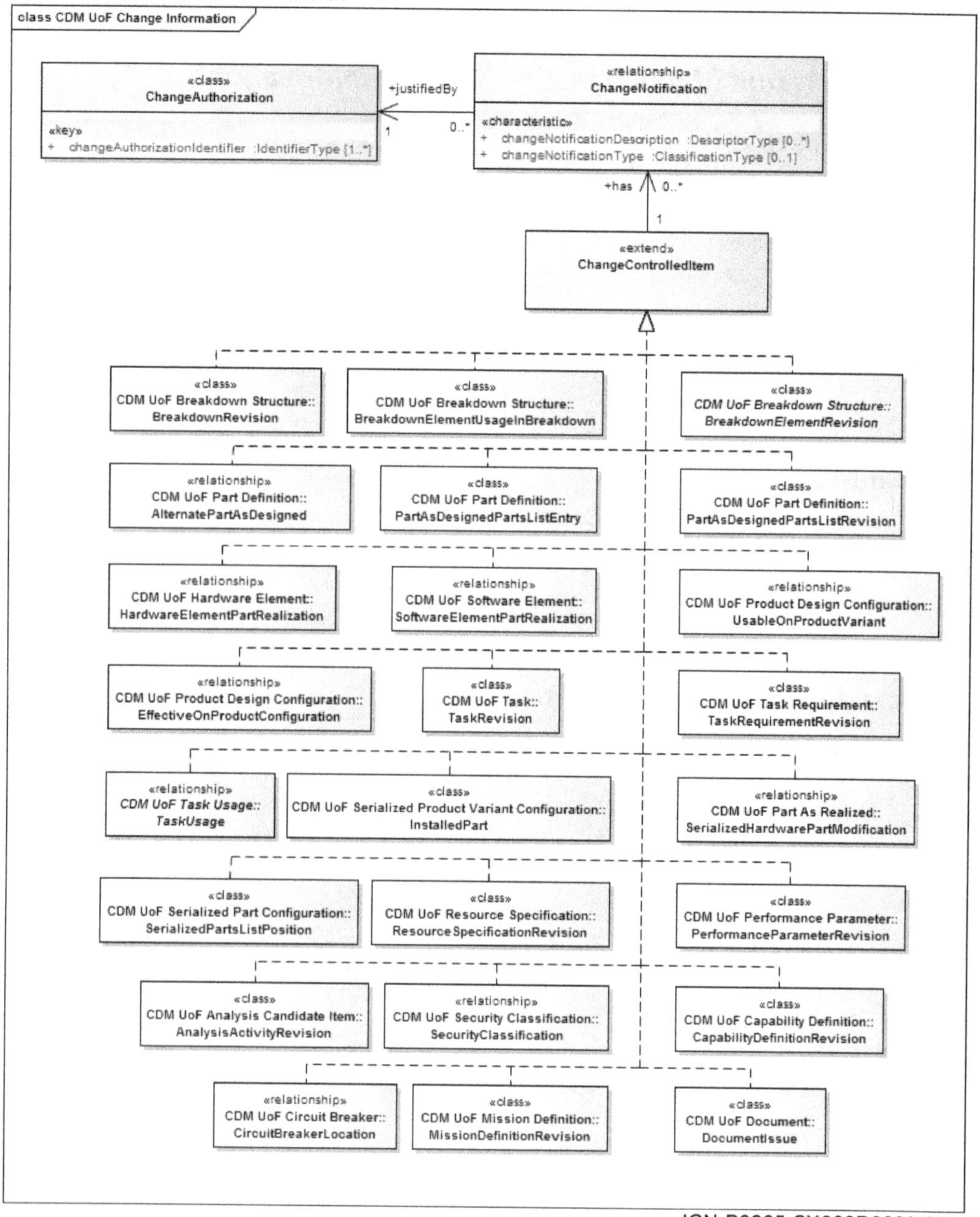

ICN-B6865-SX002D0009-003-01

Fig 1 UoF change information - UML class model

Chapter 3.8

Unit of functionality - Circuit breaker

Table of contents
Page

List of tables

List of figures

References

Table 1 References

Chap No./Document No.	Title
None	

1   Description

The circuit breaker UoF provides the capability to define circuit breakers and their locations.

2   UML class model

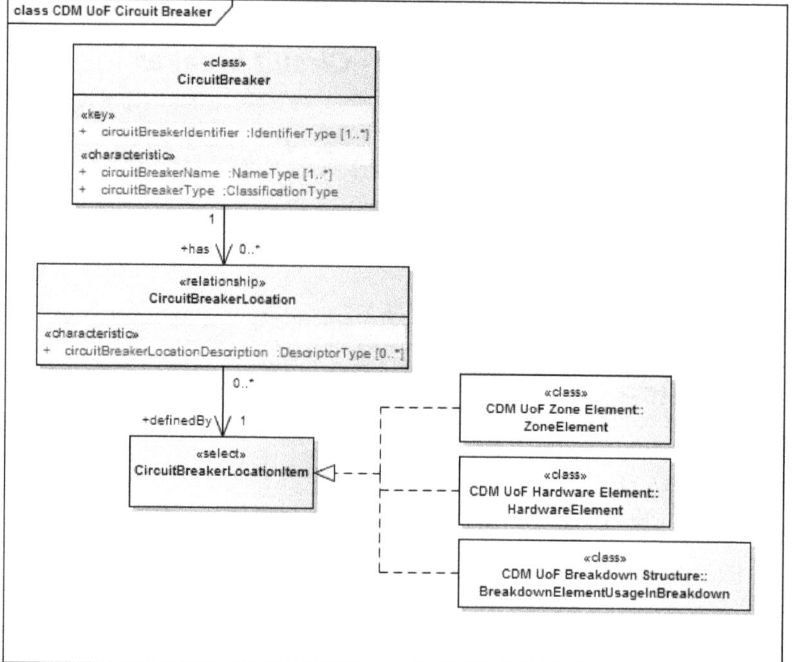

ICN-B6865-SX002D0048-001-01

Fig 1 UoF Circuit breaker - UML class model

Chapter 3.9

Unit of functionality - Competence definition

Table of contents

List of tables

List of figures

References

Table 1 References

Chap No./Document No.	Title
None	

1   Description

The competence definition UoF provides the capability to identify abilities, crafts, professions, and proficiencies.

A key feature of the UoF competence definition data model is that a competence must be defined in terms of `Skill`, `Trade` or `SkillLevel`. Refer to Fig 1.

2 UML class model

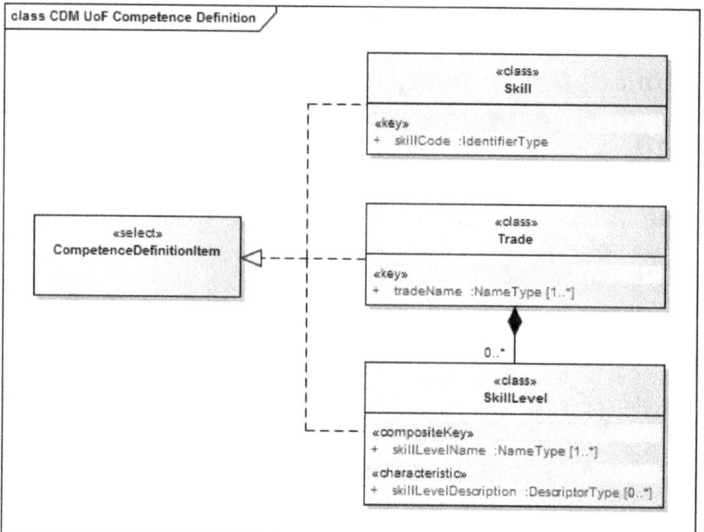

ICN-B6865-SX002D0028-001-01

Fig 1 UoF competence definition - UML class model

Chapter 3.10

Unit of functionality - Damage definition

Table of contents

List of tables

List of figures

References

Table 1 References

Chap No./Document No.	Title
Chap 3.3	Unit of functionality - Analysis candidate item
Chap 3.17	Unit of functionality - Failure mode
Chap 3.38	Unit of functionality - Special event

1   Description

The damage definition UoF provides the capability to define damages that can be induced on a Product during its in service phase.

Key features of the UoF damage definition data model (Refer to Fig 1) are:

- `DamageAnalysis` is a specialization of `AnalysisActivity` (refer to Chap 3.3) which means that `DamageDefinition` is defined in the context of an `AnalysisCandidateItem`
- A `DamageDefinition` can refer to a `SpecialEventDefinition` as its possible cause (refer to Chap 3.38)
- A `DamageDefinition` can refer to a defined `FailureMode` to give more information on the resulting consequence (refer to Chap 3.17)

2 UML class model

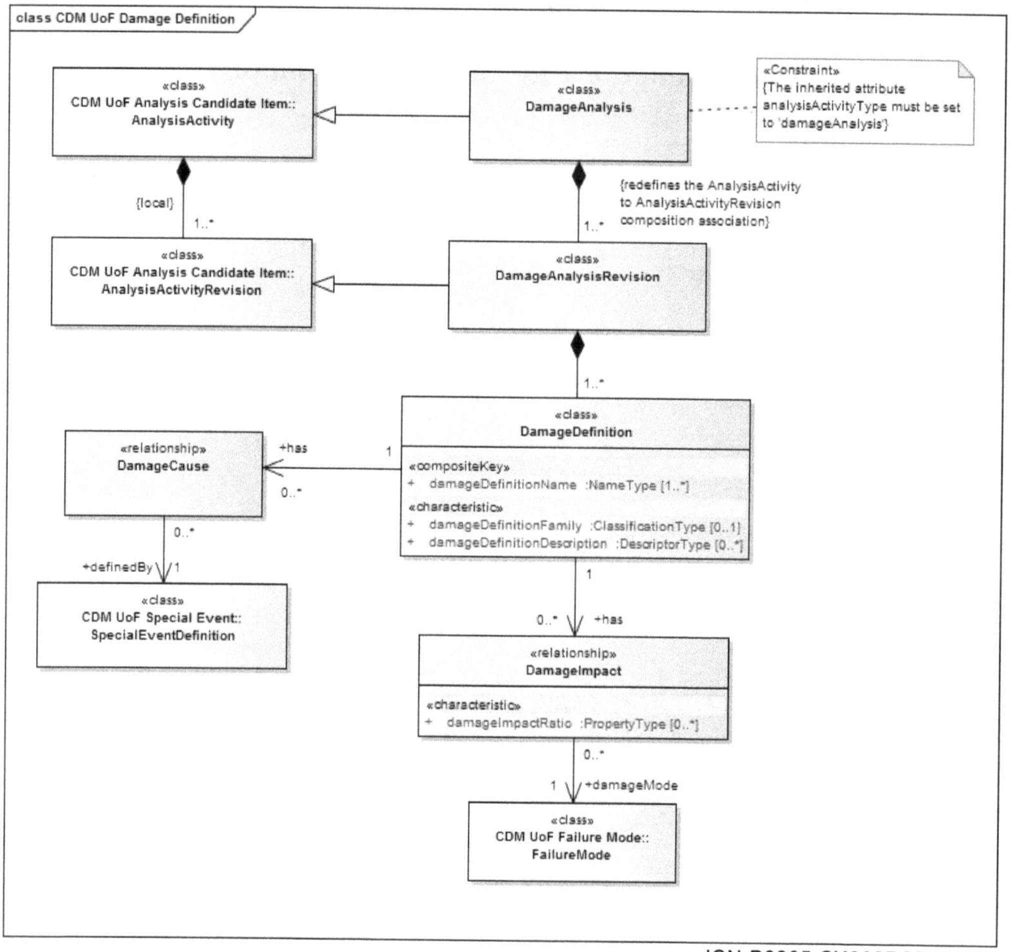

ICN-B6865-SX002D0049-001-01

Fig 1 UoF Damage definition - UML class model

Chapter 3.11

Unit of functionality - Decision tree template definition

Table of contents

List of tables

List of figures

References

Table 1 References

Chap No./Document No.	Title
None	

1   Description

The decision tree template definition UoF provides the capability to represent the definition of decision processes which must be followed when performing an actual analysis.

Key features of the UoF decision tree template definition data model (Refer to Fig 1) are:

- `DecisionTreeTemplate` is defined independently from the `DecisionTreeAnalysisItem` which means that each `DecisionTreeTemplate` can be used in multiple contexts
- Each `DecisionTreeTemplate` is made up from a set of questions (`DecisionTreeTemplateQuestionDefinition`) and actions (`DecisionTreeTemplateActionDefinition`)
- The sequence in which the questions and actions are to be performed is defined using the `DecisionTreeTemplateStartItem` for the first question or action, and the `DecisionTreeTemplateFollowOItem` for all questions and actions that follows:

2   UML class model

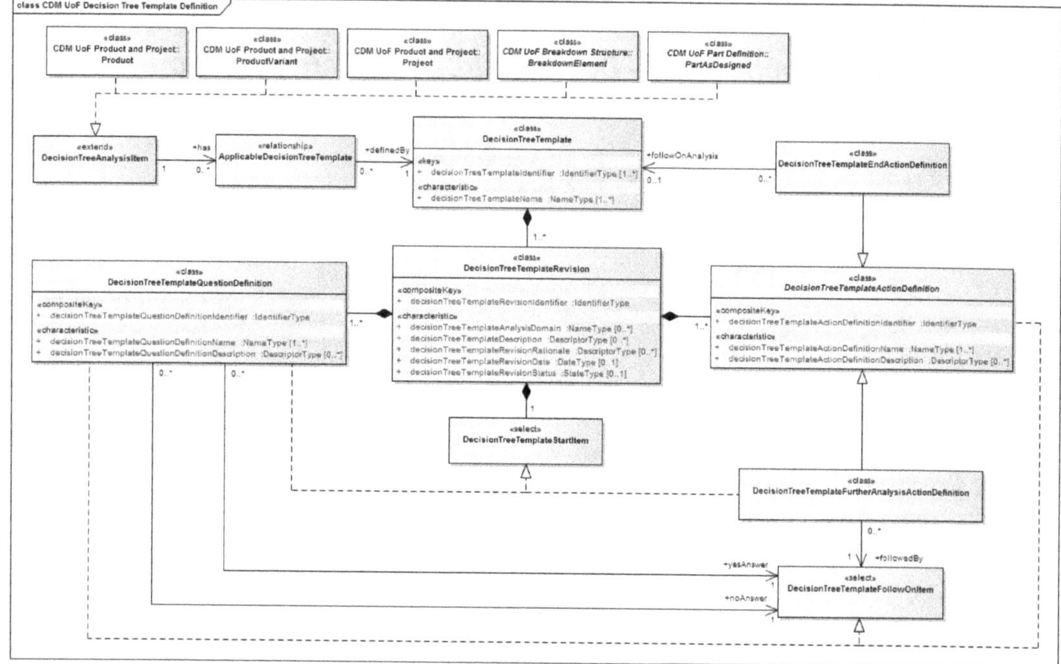

ICN-B6865-SX002D0050-001-01

Fig 1   UoF Decision tree template definition - UML class model

Chapter 3.12

Unit of functionality - Design change request

Table of contents

List of tables

List of figures

References

Table 1 References

Chap No./Document No.	Title
None	

1   Description

The design change request UoF provides the capability to identify proposed changes against an item including the rationale for each change.

2   UML class model

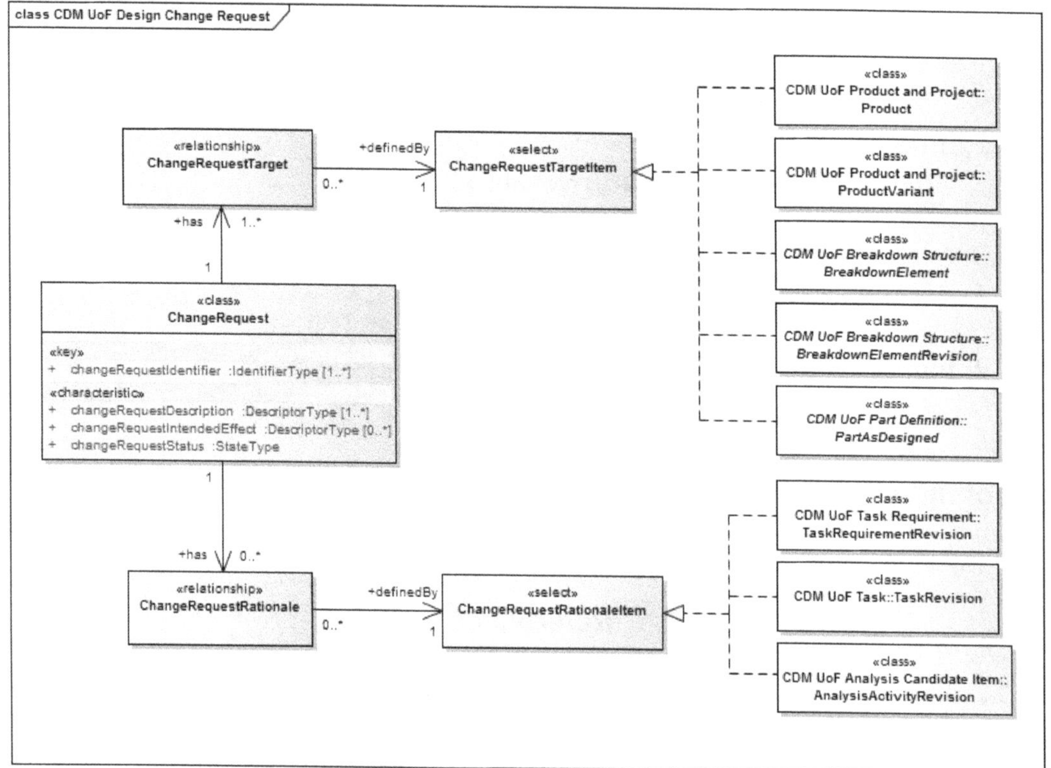

ICN-B6865-SX002D0029-002-01

Fig 1   UoF design change request - UML class model

Chapter 3.13

Unit of functionality - Digital file

Table of contents

List of tables

List of figures

References

Table 1 References

Chap No./Document No.	Title
None	

1   Description

The digital file UoF provides the capability to both refer to a digital file as well as to represent the digital file itself.

Key features of the UoF digital file data model (Refer to Fig 1) are:

- `DigitalFile` can be referenced from other classes using `ReferencedDigitalFile`
- `DigitalFile` can refer to other classes to identify items associated with the `DigitalFile` using `DigitalFileReference`

2   UML class model

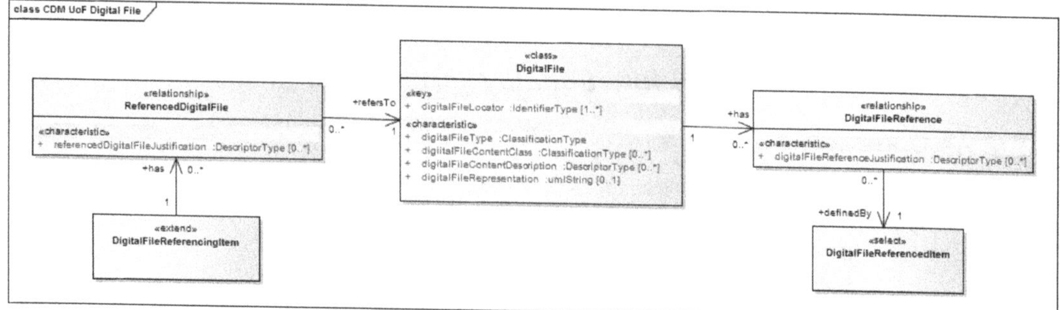

ICN-B6865-SX002D0030-001-00

Fig 1   UoF digital file - UML class model

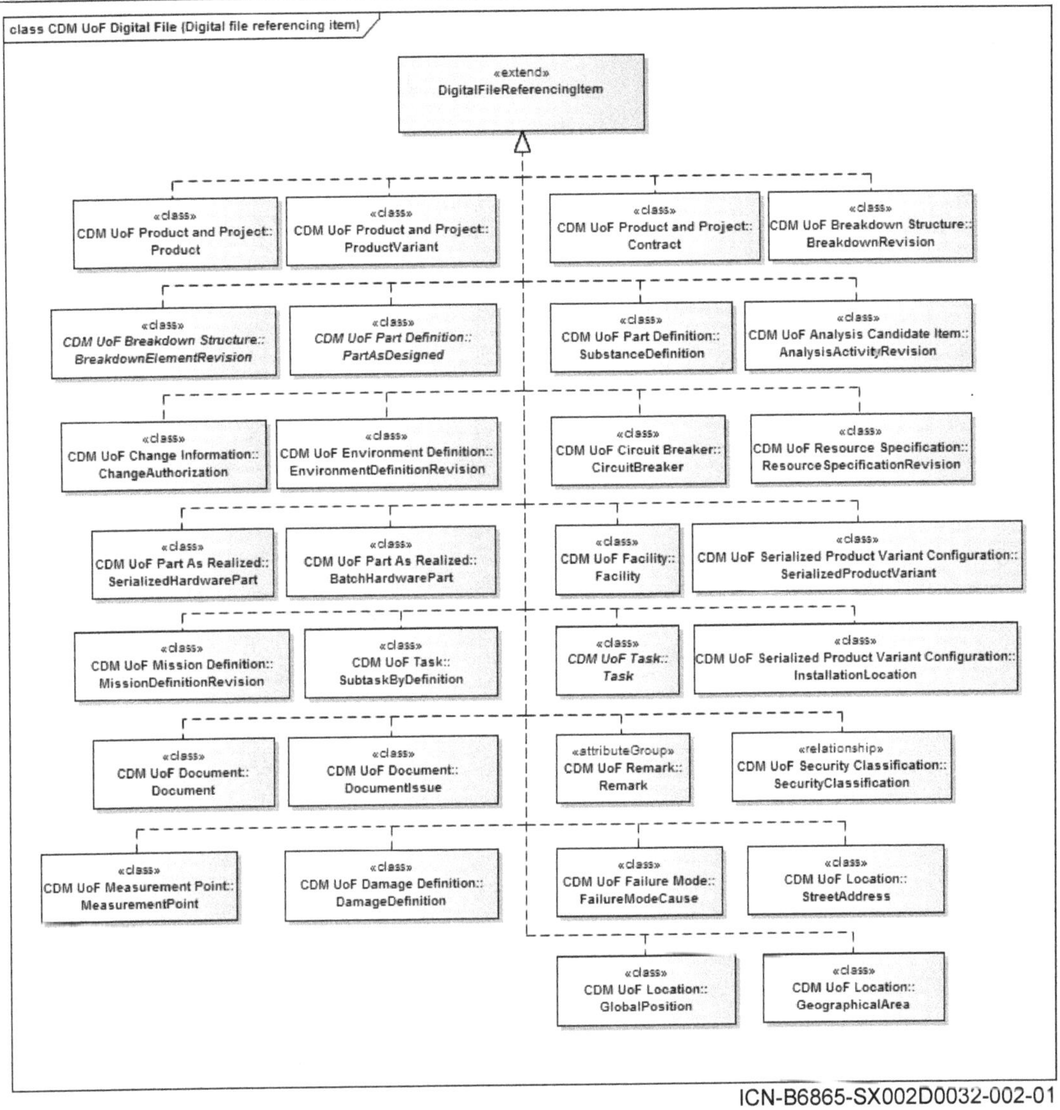

ICN-B6865-SX002D0032-002-01

Fig 2 UoF digital file - Digital file referencing item, UML class model

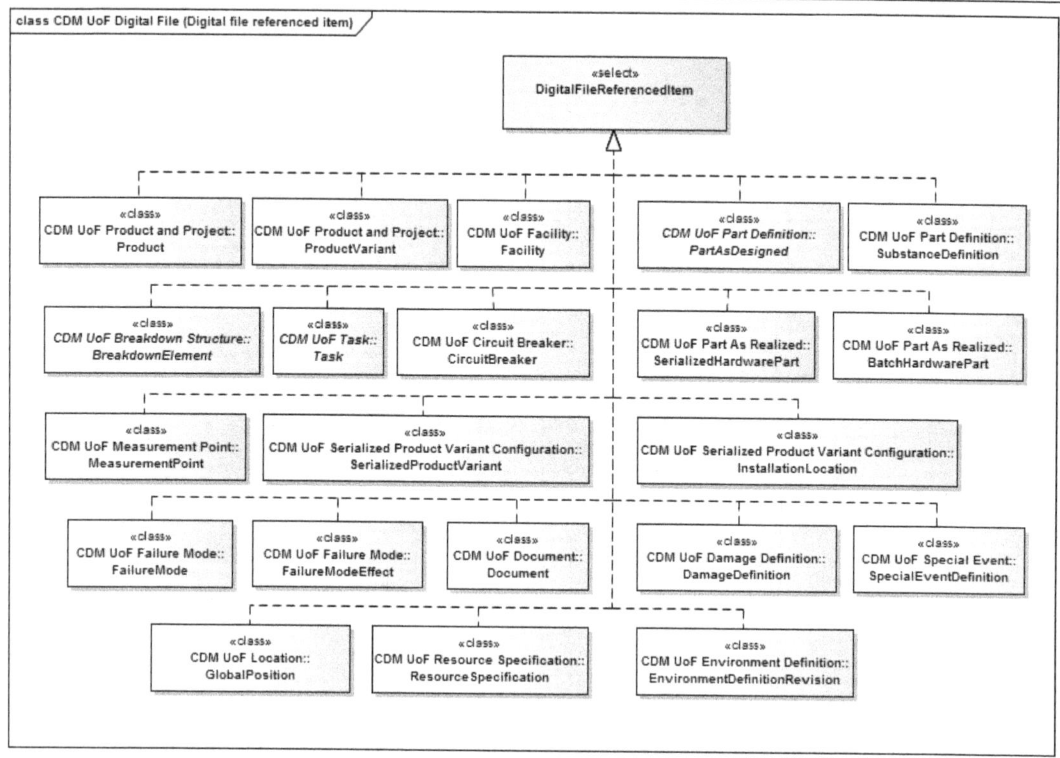

ICN-B6865-SX002D0031-003-01

Fig 3 UoF digital file - Digital file referenced item, UML class model

Chapter 3.14

Unit of functionality - Document

Table of contents
Page

List of tables

List of figures

References

Table 1 References

Chap No./Document No.	Title
None	

1   Description

The document UoF provides the capability to Identify a physical document or a digital file and their respective associated metadata.

Key features of the UoF document data model (Refer to Fig 1) are:

- A `Document` can have one or many defined `DocumentIssue`'s
- A `Document` or `DocumentIssue` can be referenced from any other class defined in the data model

2 UML class model

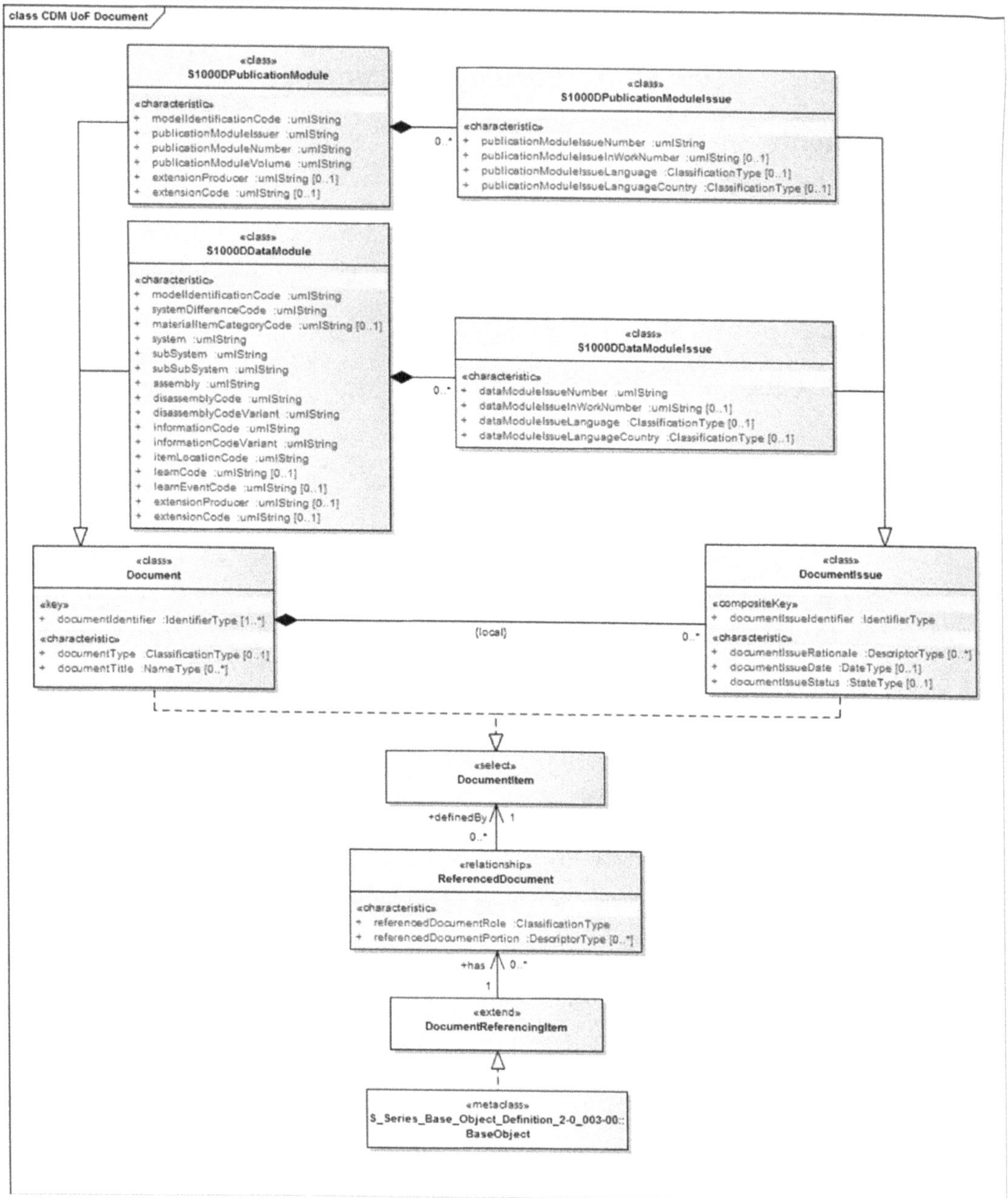

class CDM UoF Document

«class» S1000DPublicationModule
«characteristic»
+ modelIdentificationCode :umlString
+ publicationModuleIssuer :umlString
+ publicationModuleNumber :umlString
+ publicationModuleVolume :umlString
+ extensionProducer :umlString [0..1]
+ extensionCode :umlString [0..1]

«class» S1000DPublicationModuleIssue
«characteristic»
+ publicationModuleIssueNumber :umlString
+ publicationModuleIssueInWorkNumber :umlString [0..1]
+ publicationModuleIssueLanguage :ClassificationType [0..1]
+ publicationModuleIssueLanguageCountry :ClassificationType [0..1]

«class» S1000DDataModule
«characteristic»
+ modelIdentificationCode :umlString
+ systemDifferenceCode :umlString
+ materialItemCategoryCode :umlString [0..1]
+ system :umlString
+ subSystem :umlString
+ subSubSystem :umlString
+ assembly :umlString
+ disassemblyCode :umlString
+ disassemblyCodeVariant :umlString
+ informationCode :umlString
+ informationCodeVariant :umlString
+ itemLocationCode :umlString
+ learnCode :umlString [0..1]
+ learnEventCode :umlString [0..1]
+ extensionProducer :umlString [0..1]
+ extensionCode :umlString [0..1]

«class» S1000DDataModuleIssue
«characteristic»
+ dataModuleIssueNumber :umlString
+ dataModuleIssueInWorkNumber :umlString [0..1]
+ dataModuleIssueLanguage :ClassificationType [0..1]
+ dataModuleIssueLanguageCountry :ClassificationType [0..1]

«class» Document
«key»
+ documentIdentifier :IdentifierType [1..*]
«characteristic»
+ documentType :ClassificationType [0..1]
+ documentTitle :NameType [0..*]

«class» DocumentIssue
«compositeKey»
+ documentIssueIdentifier :IdentifierType
«characteristic»
+ documentIssueRationale :DescriptorType [0..*]
+ documentIssueDate :DateType [0..1]
+ documentIssueStatus :StateType [0..1]

«select» DocumentItem

«relationship» ReferencedDocument
«characteristic»
+ referencedDocumentRole :ClassificationType
+ referencedDocumentPortion :DescriptorType [0..*]

«extend» DocumentReferencingItem

«metaclass» S_Series_Base_Object_Definition_2-0_003-00::BaseObject

ICN-B6865-SX002D0033-002-01

Fig 1 UoF document - UML class model

Chapter 3.15

Unit of functionality - Environment definition

Table of contents

List of tables

List of figures

References

Table 1 References

Chap No./Document No.	Title
None	

1   Description

The environment definition UoF provides the capability to define circumstances, objects, events and/or conditions by which something can be surrounded and that influence the performance of an associated item.

Key features of the UoF environment definition data model (Refer to Fig 1) are:

- Each associated `EnvironmentDefinitionItem` can have zero, one or many associated `EnvironmentDefintion`'s
- Each `EnvironmentDefintion` can have zero, one or many documented characteristics

2   UML class model

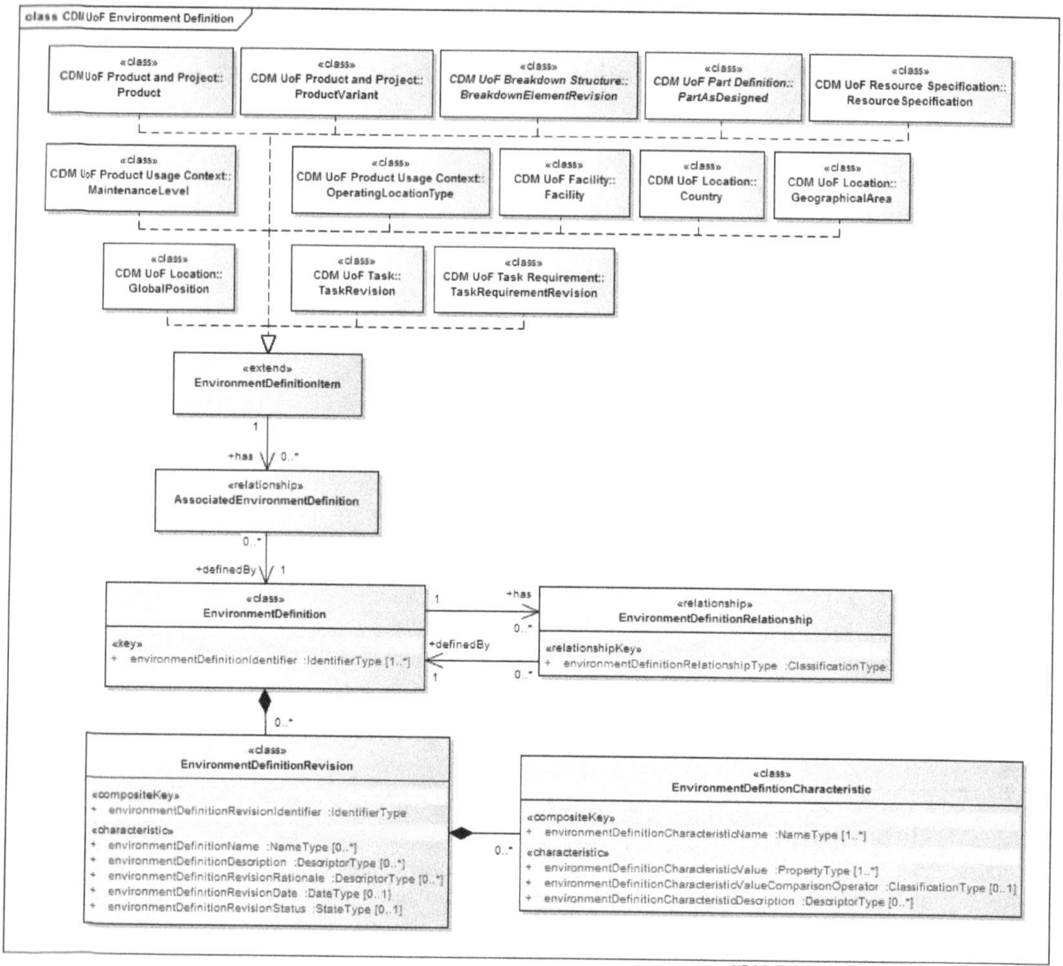

ICN-B6865-SX002D0051-001-01

Fig 1   UoF Environment definition - UML class model

Chapter 3.16

Unit of functionality - Facility

Table of contents
Page

List of tables

List of figures

References

Table 1 References

Chap No./Document No.	Title
Chap 3.20	Unit of functionality - Location
Chap 3.33	Unit of functionality - Resource specification

1   Description

The facility UoF provides the capability to identify a facility and to declare to what extent it fulfills a set of identified infrastructure requirements.

Key features of the UoF facility data model (Refer to Fig 1) are:

- `Facility` and its compliancy can be associated with infrastructure resource requirements which are identified during task analysis activities (refer to Chap 3.33)
- `Facility` can be associated with a `LocationItem` (refer to Chap 3.20) and a `FacilityOperatior`
- `Facility` must represent either a `MaintenanceFacility` or an `OperatingBase`

2 UML class model

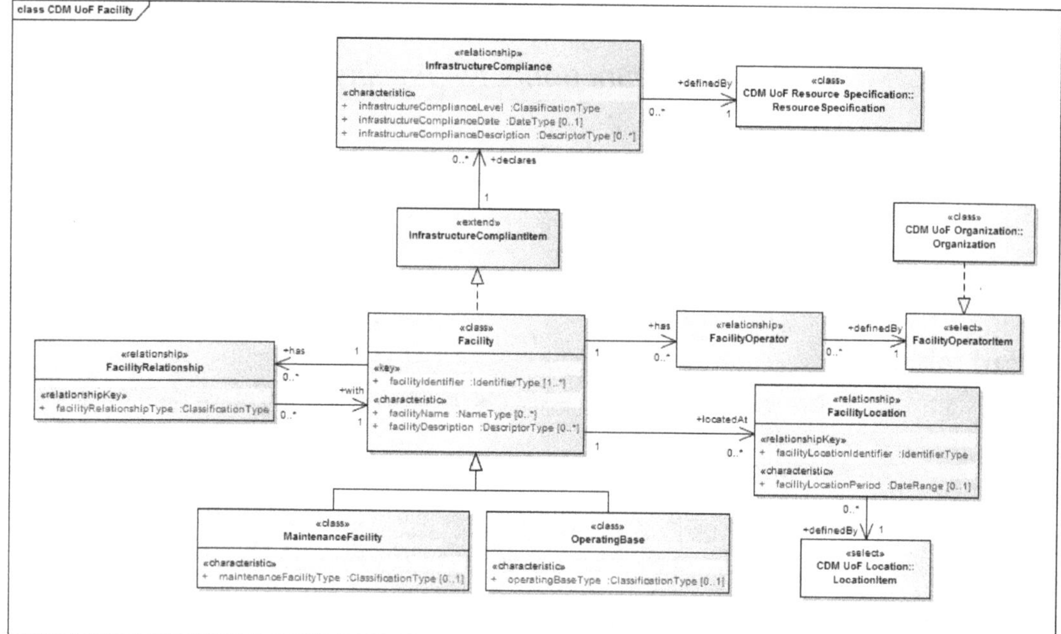

ICN-B6865-SX002D0034-002-01

Fig 1 UoF Facility - UML class model

Chapter 3.17

Unit of functionality - Failure mode

Table of contents

Page

List of tables

List of figures

References

Table 1 References

Chap No./Document No.	Title
Chap 3.5	Unit of functionality - Breakdown structure
Chap 3.26	Unit of functionality - Part definition

1   Description

The failure mode UoF provides the capability to define the failure modes, their causes and effects.

Key features of the UoF failure mode data model (Refer to Fig 1) are:

- `FailureModeAnalysis` can be defined in the context of a `BreakdownElement`, `BreakdownElementRevision` (refer to Chap 3.5) or `PartAsDesigned` (refer to Chap 3.26).
- Both technical, system, and function `FailureModeAnalysis` can be documented using the failure mode data model
- An instance of `FailureMode` can explicitly refer to a `FailureModeCauseItem` in order to eg, document `FailureMode`'s that can occur as a consequence of another `FailureMode`
- An instance of `FailureModeEffect` can explicitly refer to a `FailureModeEffectItem` which allows for a more granular documentation of `FailureModeEffect`'s

2 UML class model

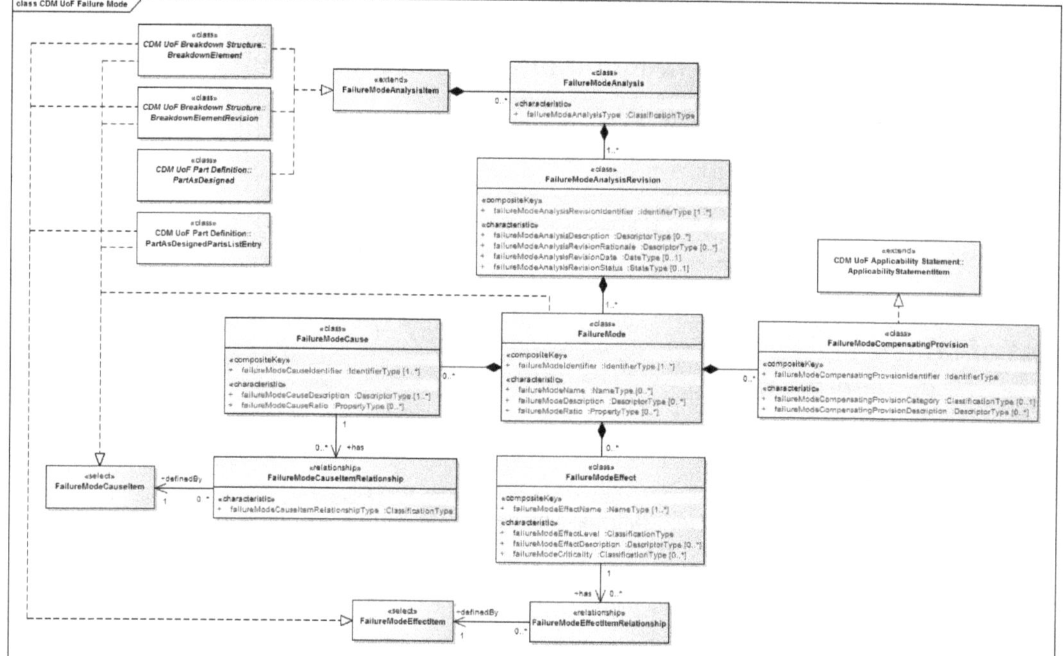

ICN-B6865-SX002D0052-001-01

Fig 1 UoF Failure mode - UML class model

Chapter 3.18

Unit of functionality - Hardware element

Table of contents

List of tables

List of figures

References

Table 1 References

Chap No./Document No.	Title
Chap 3.5	Unit of functionality - Breakdown structure
Chap 3.26	Unit of functionality - Part definition

1   Description

The hardware element UoF provides the capability to specify that an element within a breakdown is hardware and can be associated with the hardware part(s) that fulfill its requirements.

Key features of the UoF hardware element data model (Refer to Fig 1) are:

- `HardwareElement` is a specialization of `BreakdownElement` (refer to Chap 3.5) which means that, wherever `BreakdownElement` is being used in the data model, `HardwareElement` can be used instead
- `HardwareElementRevision` is a specialization of `BreakdownElementRevision` which means that, wherever `BreakdownElementRevision` is being used in the data model, `HardwareElementRevision` can be used instead
- An instance of `HardwareElementRevision` can be associated with one or many instances of `HardwarePartAsDesigned` (refer to Chap 3.26) that meet the requirements and specification for the `HardwareElement`

2 UML class model

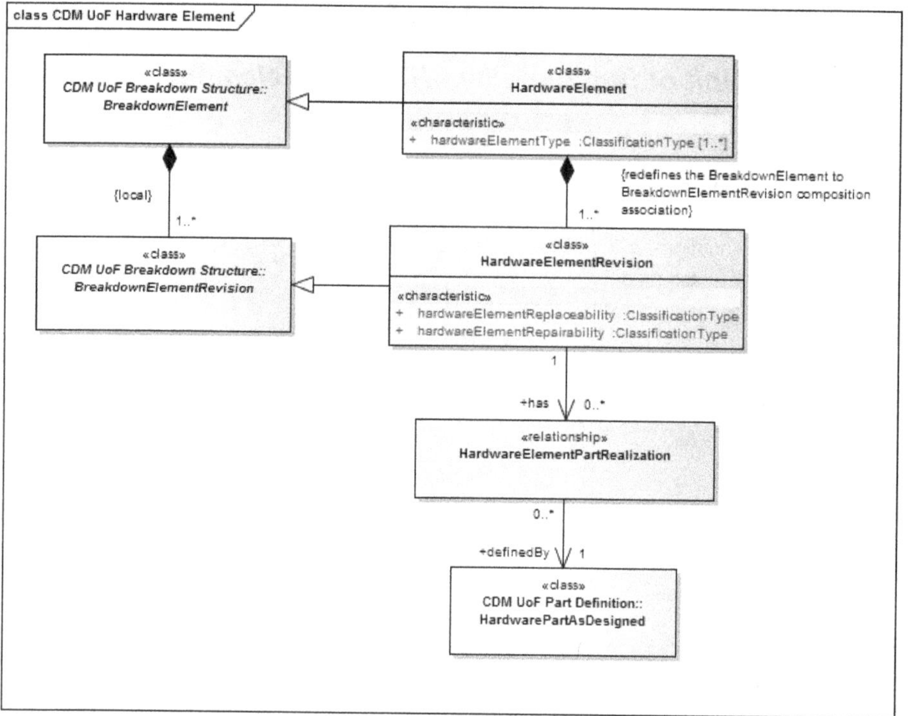

ICN-B6865-SX002D0005-003-01

Fig 1 UoF hardware element - UML class model

Chapter 3.19

Unit of functionality - In service optimization analysis

Table of contents

List of tables

List of figures

References

Table 1 References

Chap No./Document No.	Title
Chap 3.11	Unit of functionality - Decision tree template definition

1   Description

The in service optimization analysis UoF provides the capability to represent the result from an actual analysis carried out for the analyzed item and in accordance with a defined `DecisionTreeTemplate` (refer to Chap 3.11).

Key features of the UoF in service optimization analysis data model (Refer to Fig 1) are:

- Answers (`QuestionInServiceOptimizationAnalysisStep`) and actions (`FurtherAnalysisInServiceOptimizationAnalysisStep` and `FinalInServiceOptimizationAnalysisStep`) resulting from a specific in service optimization analysis are organized in chronological order with references to its respective question (`DecisionTreeTemplateQuestionDefinition`) and action (`DecisionTreeTemplateFurtherAnalysisActionDefinition` and `DecisionTreeTemplateEndActionDefinition`) defined in the `DecisionTreeTemplate` (refer to Chap 3.11).

2   UML class model

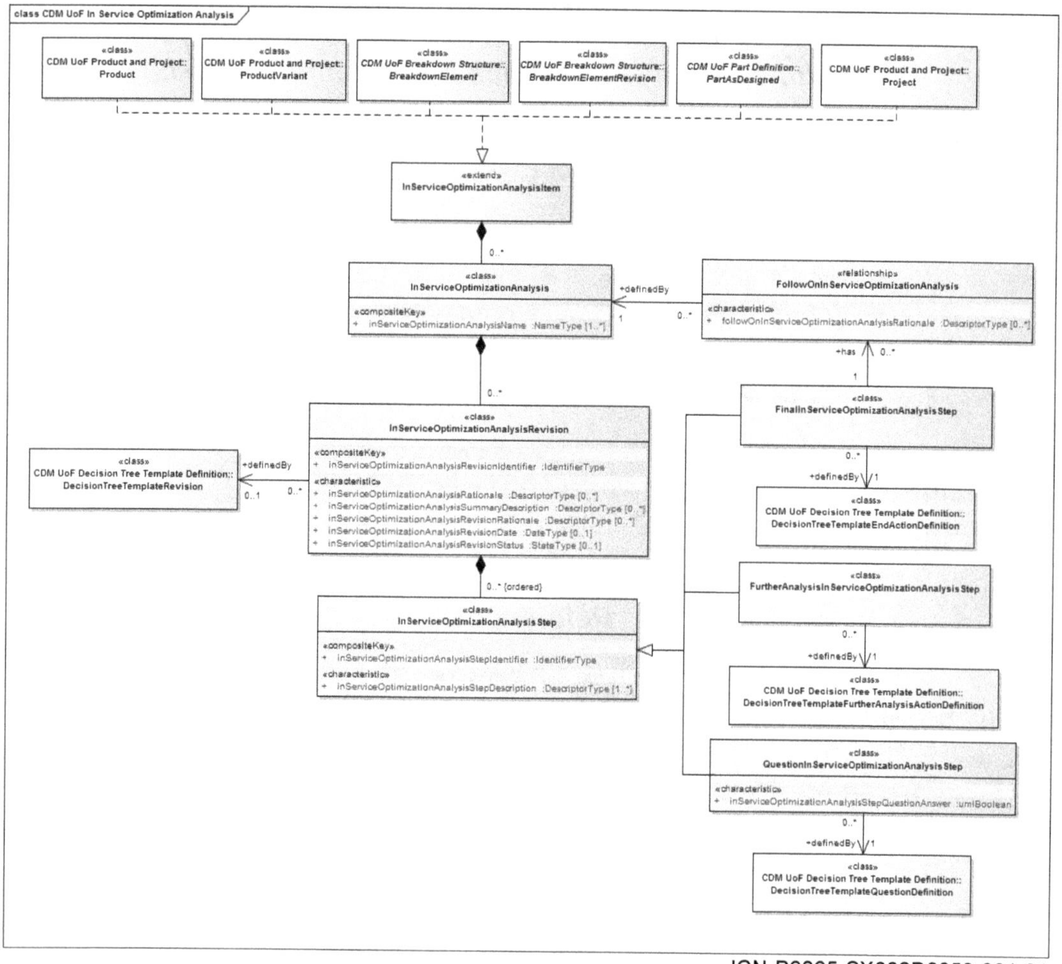

ICN-B6865-SX002D0053-001-01

Fig 1 UoF In service optimization analysis - UML class model

Chapter 3.20

Unit of functionality - Location

Table of contents

Page

List of tables

List of figures

References

Table 1 References

Chap No./Document No.	Title
None	

1   Description

The location UoF provides the capability to define a geographically locatable position.

A key feature of the UoF location data model is that a `Location` must be defined as `Country`, `StreetAddress`, `GeographicArea` or `GlobalPosition`. Refer to Fig 1.

2   UML class model

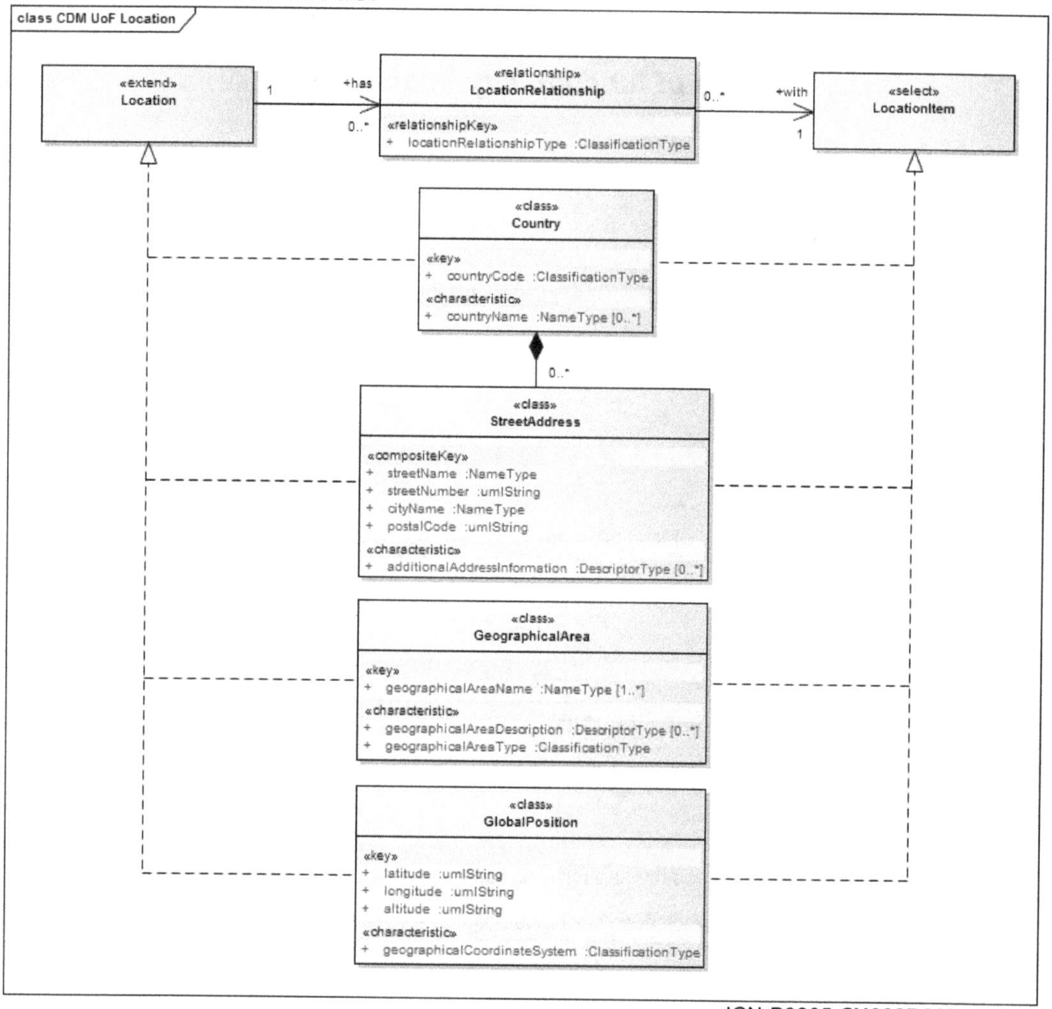

ICN-B6865-SX002D0035-003-01

Fig 1 UoF Location - UML class model

Chapter 3.21

Unit of functionality - Measurement point

Table of contents
Page

List of tables

List of figures

References

Table 1 References

Chap No./Document No.	Title
None	

1   Description

The measurement point UoF provides the capability to record measured values for its associated item.

2   UML class model

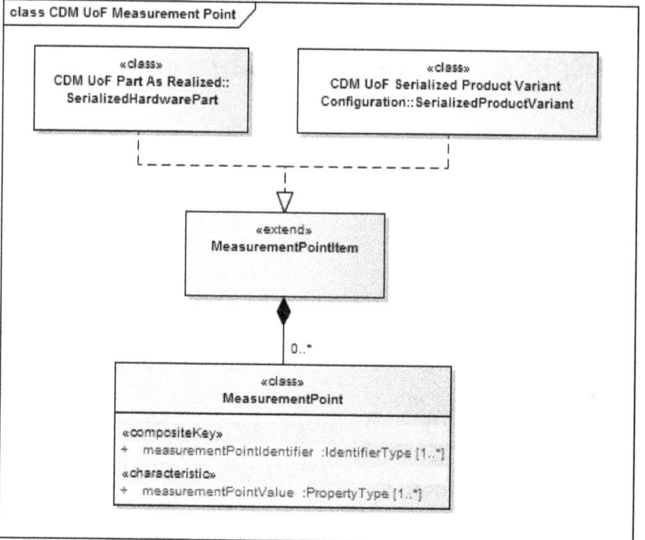

ICN-B6865-SX002D0054-001-01

Fig 1 UoF Measurement point - UML class model

Chapter 3.22

Unit of functionality - Message

Table of contents

List of tables

List of figures

References

Table 1 References

Chap No./Document No.	Title
None	

1   Description

The message UoF provides the capability to identify a collection of information which is communicated from one party to another.

Key features of the UoF message data model (Refer to Fig 1) are:

- `MessageContext` provides the context within which the `Message` is defined
- `MessageContent` must be specialized in order to represent the collection of information that is the subject for the `Message`
- `MessageParty` which identifies its stakeholders, eg, sender and receiver

2 UML class model

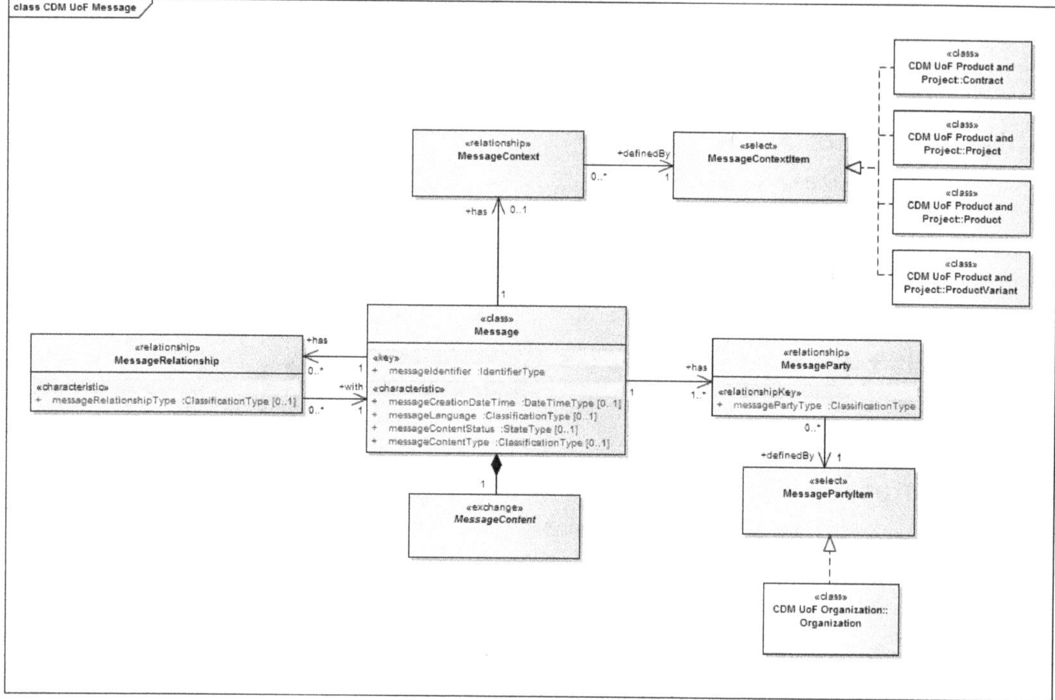

ICN-B6865-SX002D0021-004-01

Fig 1 UoF Message - UML class model

Chapter 3.23

Unit of functionality - Mission definition

Table of contents

List of tables

List of figures

References

Table 1 References

Chap No./Document No.	Title
None	

1   Description

The mission definition UoF supports the definition of operational scenarios to be carried out by a Product.

Example:

Examples of `MissionDefinition` are search and rescue, troop transport and long haul flight.

2 UML class model

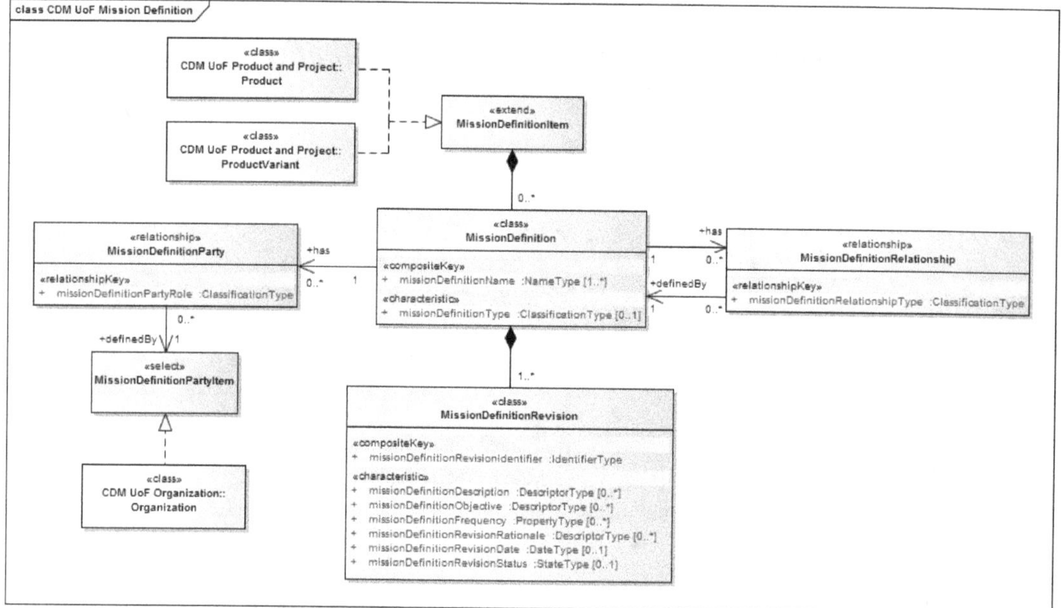

ICN-B6865-SX002D0055-001-01

Fig 1 UoF Mission definition - UML class model

Chapter 3.24

Unit of functionality - Organization

Table of contents

List of tables

List of figures

References

Table 1 References

Chap No./Document No.	Title
None	

1   Description

The organization UoF provides the capability to identify `Organization`'s.

2   UML class model

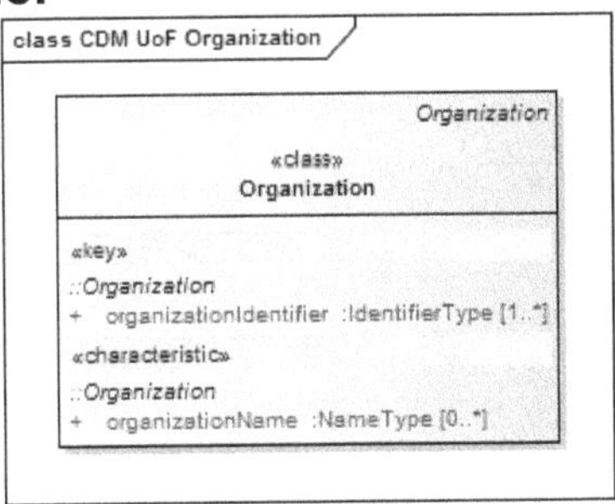

ICN-B6865-SX002D0036-001-01

Fig 1 UoF Organization - UML class model

Page intentionally blank.

Chapter 3.25

Unit of functionality - Part as realized

Table of contents
Page

List of tables

List of figures

References

Table 1 References

Chap No./Document No.	Title
None	

1   Description

The part as realized UoF provides the capability to identify actual existing parts.

A key feature of the UoF part as realized data model is that a part as realized is defined as either `SerializedHardwarePart`, `BatchHardwarePart` or `SoftwarePartAsRealized`. **Refer to** Fig 1.

2   UML class model

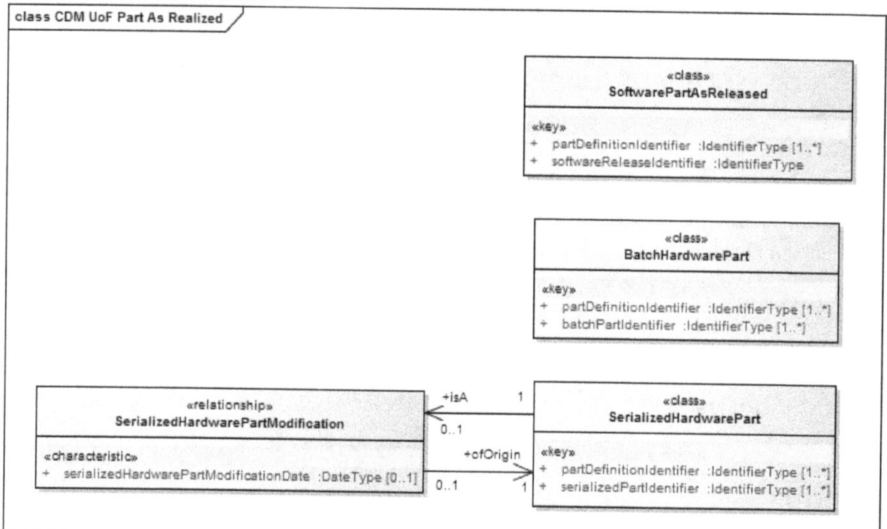

ICN-B6865-SX002D0037-003-01

Fig 1 UoF part as realized - UML class model

Chapter 3.26

Unit of functionality - Part definition

Table of contents

List of tables

List of figures

References

Table 1 References

Chap No./Document No.	Title
None	

1   Description

The part definition UoF provides the capability to define hardware and software parts, their characteristics, and associated parts lists.

Key features of the UoF part definition data model (Refer to Fig 1) are:

- A `PartAsDesigned` represents the definitional information for an artifact fulfilling a set of requirements, which can be produced or realized
  A `PartAsDesigned` must be defined as either a `HardwarePartAsDesigned` or a `SoftwarePartAsDesigned`
- A `PartAsDesigned` can have one or more alternate `PartAsDesigned`. An alternate `PartAsDesigned` is interchangeable with the base `PartAsDesigned` in all its usages
- A `PartAsDesigned` can have one or many Bill-Of-Materials (BOM) using the `PartAsDesignedPartsList` class, ie, a `PartAsDesigned` can consist of other `PartAsDesigned`
- An entry in a `PartAsDesignedPartsList` can have one or many substitute parts
- A substitute part is only valid in the context of its usage within the specified `PartAsDesignedPartsListRevision`.
- A `HardwarePartAsDesigned` can contain substances. `SubstanceDefinition`'s are defined separately and are then associated with the `HardwarePartAsDesigned` in which they are being contained

2 UML class model

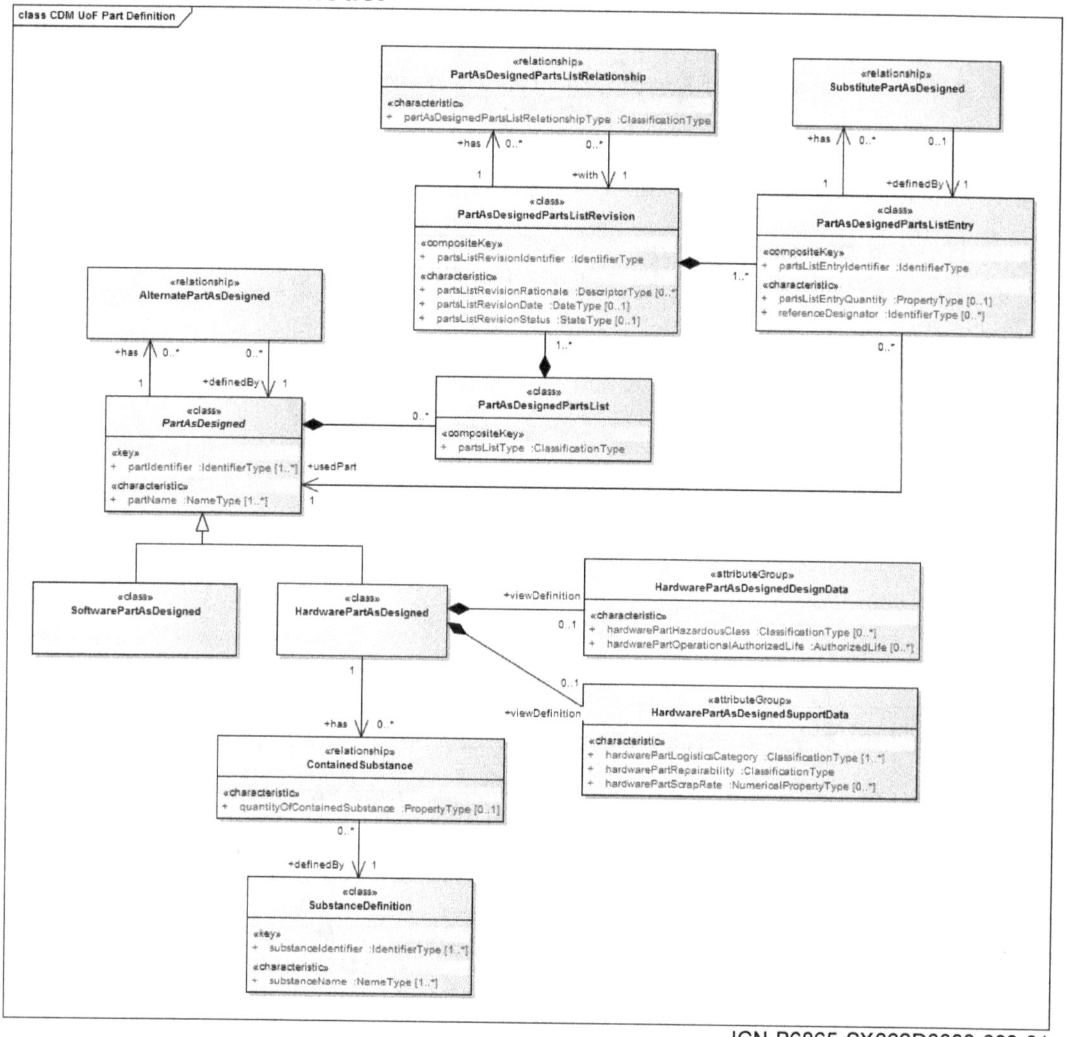

ICN-B6865-SX002D0003-003-01

Fig 1 UoF part definition - UML class model

Chapter 3.27

Unit of functionality - Performance parameter

Table of contents
Page

List of tables

List of figures

References

Table 1 References

Chap No./Document No.	Title
None	

1 Description

The performance parameter UoF supports the definition of metrics that if changed will have a major impact on the system performance, schedule, cost and/or risk.

Key features of the UoF performance parameter data model (Refer to Fig 1) are:

- A `performanceParameterValue` can have additional characterizations besides the characterizations that are associated with `PropertyType`. These additional characterizations are `performanceParameterValueFraction` and `performanceParameterCalculationMethod`

2   UML class model

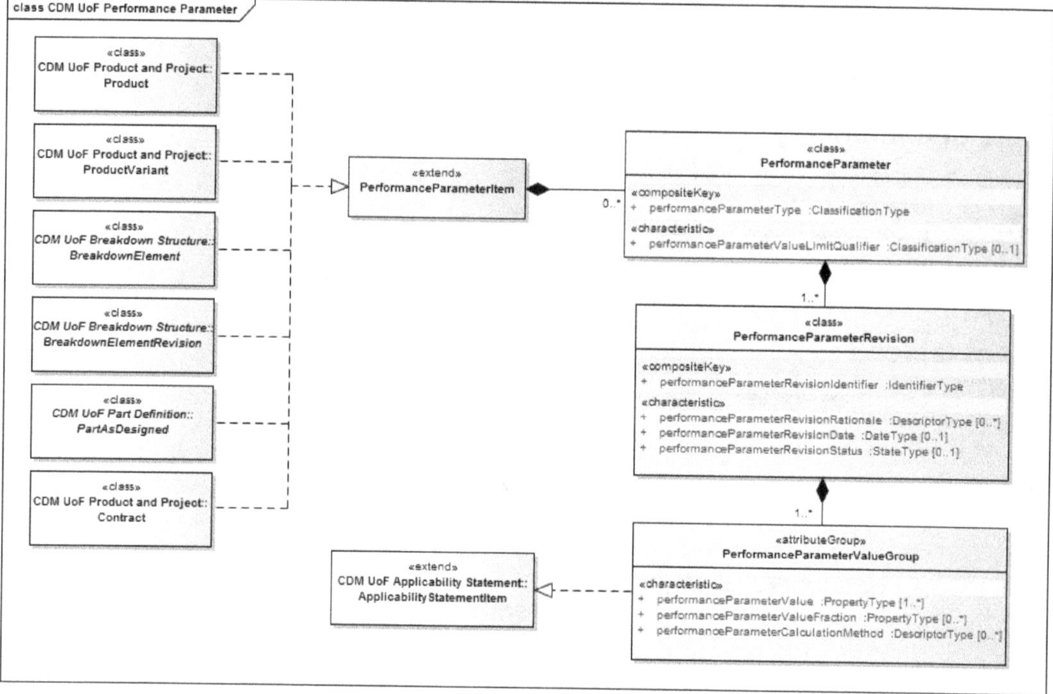

ICN-B6865-SX002D0056-001-01

Fig 1 UoF Performance parameter - UML class model

Chapter 3.28

Unit of functionality - Product and project

Table of contents

Page

List of tables

List of figures

References

Table 1 References

Chap No./Document No.	Title
Chap 3.28	Unit of functionality - Product and project

1   Description

The product and project UoF provides the capability to identify the Product(s) which are in focus for an Integrated Product Support (IPS) program.

The product and project UoF also allows for defining additional project and contract information related to the IPS program.

Key features of the UoF product and project data model (Refer to Fig 1) are:

- There must be at least one defined ProductVariant for each Product
- Projects can be related to one or many Contract's, which in turn can be organized into a chain of associated Contract's eg, subcontracts
- Each Contract can be associated with a set of ContractParty eg, customer and contractor
- Each Contract must identify one or many ContractedItem's eg, Product's or ProductVariant's (refer to Chap 3.28)
- Each identified ContractedItem can also include information on the quantity of contracted items

2 UML class model

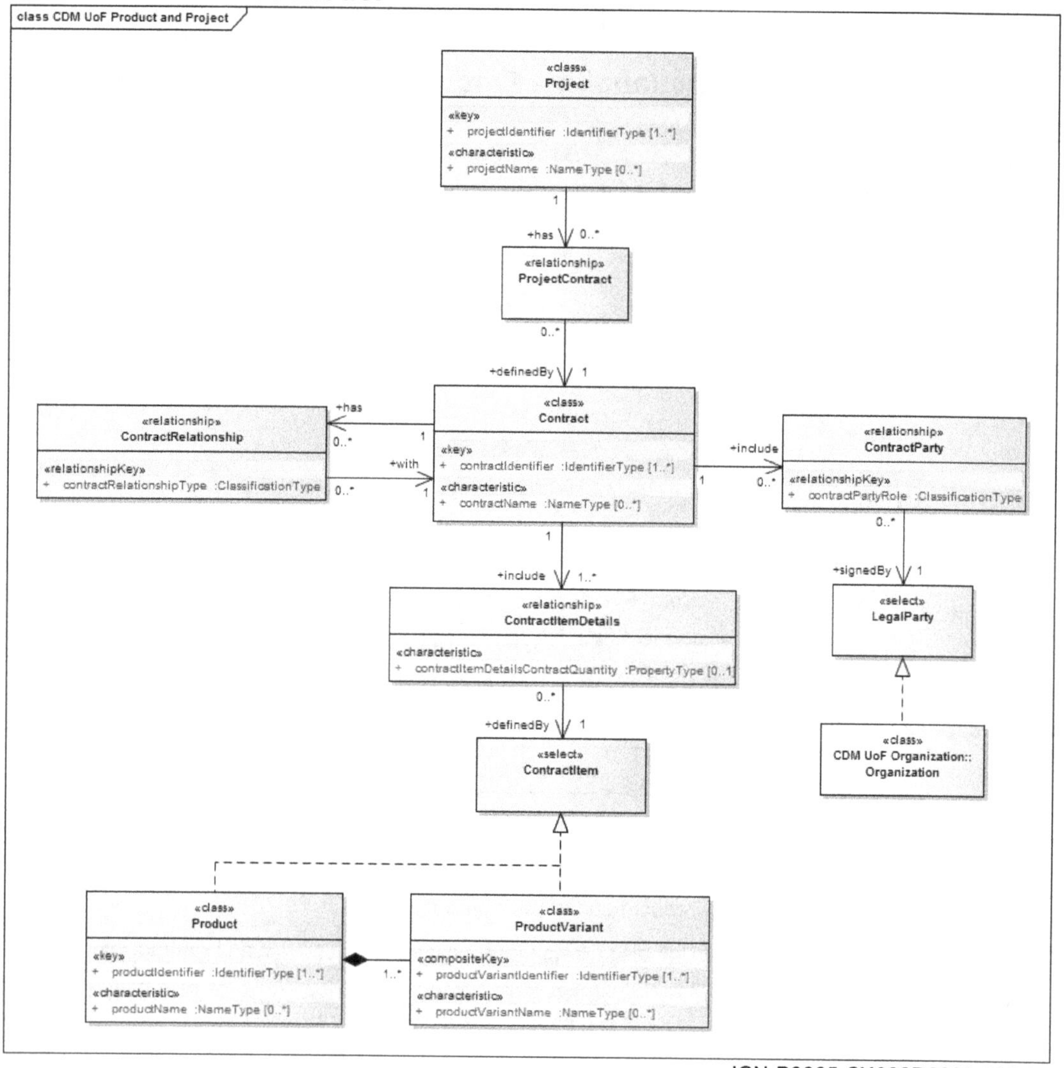

ICN-B6865-SX002D0020-003-01

Fig 1 UoF product and project - UML class model

Chapter 3.29

Unit of functionality - Product design configuration

Table of contents

Page

List of tables

List of figures

References

Table 1 References

Chap No./Document No.	Title
Chap 3.4	Unit of functionality - Applicability statement
Chap 3.5	Unit of functionality - Breakdown structure
Chap 3.26	Unit of functionality - Part definition
Chap 3.28	Unit of functionality - Product and project
ISO 10303	Standard for the Exchange of Product Model Data
SAE-GEIA-STD-0007	Logistics Product Data

1   Description

The product design configuration UoF provides the capability to define permitted combinations of breakdown elements and parts as designed, in the context of product variants and `AllowedProductConfiguration`'s.

Key features of the UoF product design configuration data model (Refer to Fig 1) are:

- A `ProductVariant` (refer to Chap 3.28) can be filtered out from the `Breakdown` structure (refer to Chap 3.5) defined for the `Product` using `UsableOnProductVariant`
- A `ProductVariant` can be further refined into specific `AllowedProductConfiguration`'s, which defines permitted combinations of hardware and software parts which can or must be installed in specific locations (positions),

and demonstrates that a product complies with design requirements or applicable regulations

- An `AllowedProductConfiguration` can either be defined as a part numbered item (`AllowedProductConfigurationHarwarePartAsDesigned`) and have its explicit `PartAsDesignedPartsList` (refer to <u>Chap 3.26</u>), or be defined in terms of an `AllowedProductConfigurationByConfigurationIdentifier` where permitted combinations of hardware and software parts is defined in relationship to the `Breakdown` structure for the a given `ProductVariant`
- Items included in the definition of a `Breakdown` structure or a `PartAsDesignedPartsList` can be restricted to specific end item serial number ranges

Note

Standards such as ISO 10303 often use the term effectivity to describe product design related restrictions, where the restriction defines the allowed usage of components in the context of a particular product configuration.

Note

A `ProductVariant` can either have its own uniquely identified `Breakdown` structure(s) or be filtered out from the `Breakdown` structure(s) defined for the `Product` using `UsableOnProductVariant`. This concept is also known as System/End Item Usable On Code in SAE-GEIA-STD-0007.

Note

`UsableOnProductVariant` and `AllowedProductConfiguration` are used to define restrictions for a given product design (product definition), whereas `ApplicabilityStatement` (refer to <u>Chap 3.4</u>) is used to define usage related restrictions.

2 UML class model

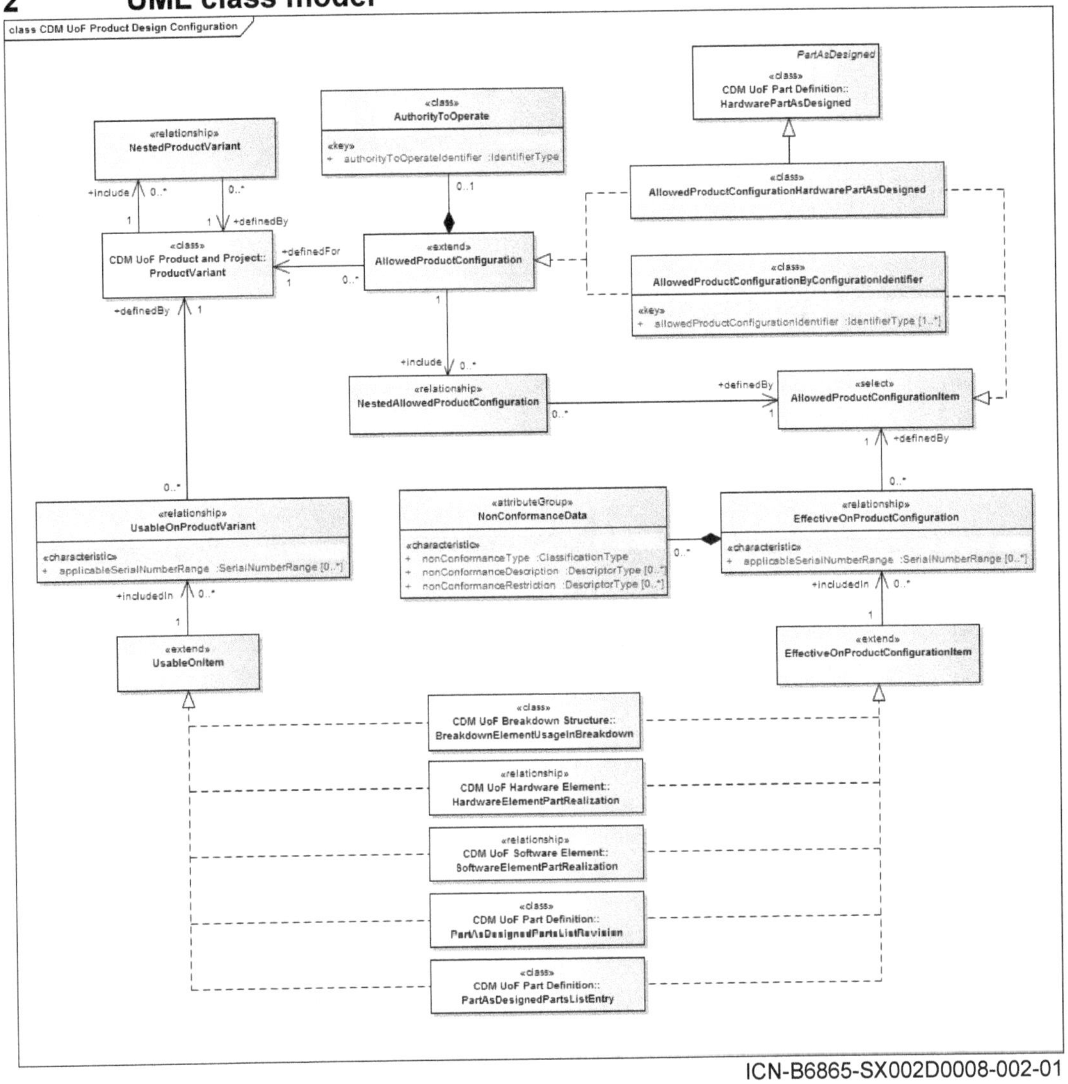

Fig 1 UoF product design configuration - UML class model

ICN-B6865-SX002D0008-002-01

SX002D-A-03-29-0000-00A-040A-A

Page intentionally blank.

Chapter 3.30

Unit of functionality - Product usage context

Table of contents

Page

List of tables

List of figures

References

Table 1 References

Chap No./Document No.	Title
Chap 3.28	Unit of functionality - Product and project

1   Description

The product usage context UoF provides the capability to define the context in which the defined `Product`(s) and `ProductVariant`(s) (refer to Chap 3.28) are to be operated and maintained.

2   UML class model

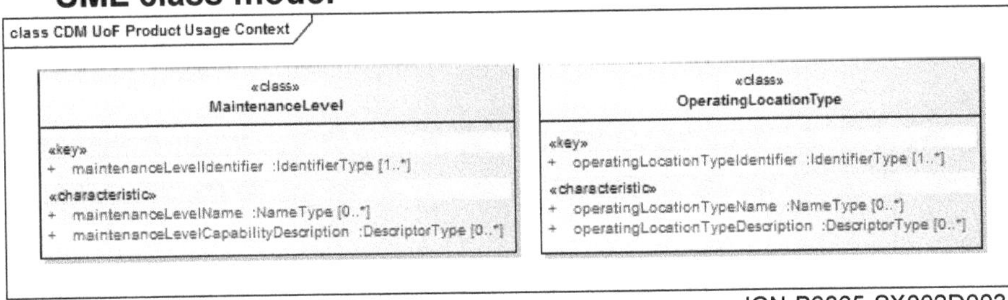

ICN-B6865-SX002D0038-001-01

Fig 1 UoF product usage context - UML class model

Page intentionally blank.

Chapter 3.31

Unit of functionality - Product usage phase

Table of contents

List of tables

List of figures

References

Table 1 References

Chap No./Document No.	Title
None	

1   Description

The product usage phase UoF defines periods of time during which a Product is in an operational state which has specific characteristics that need special considerations. Refer to Fig 1.

Example:

Examples of `ProductUsagePhase` are preflight, postflight, cruise, taxiing for an aircraft, and emersion, surface and dock for a submarine

2 UML class model

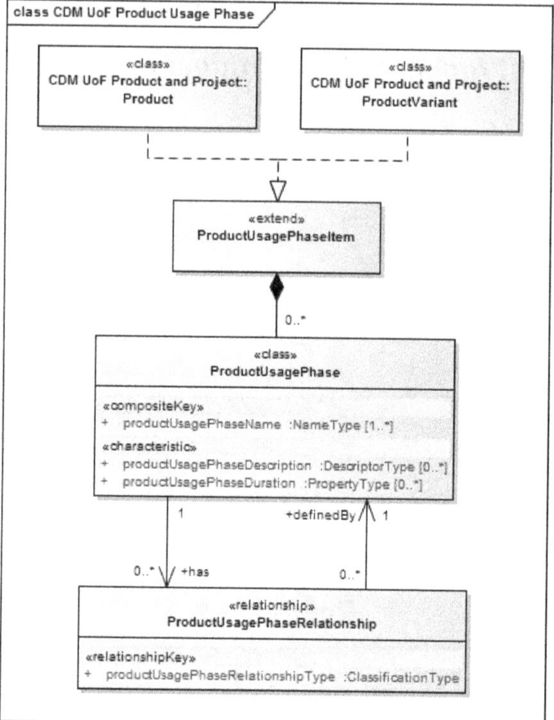

ICN-B6865-SX002D0057-001-01

Fig 1 UoF Product usage phase - UML class model

Chapter 3.32

Unit of functionality - Remark

Table of contents

List of tables

List of figures

References

Table 1 References

Chap No./Document No.	Title
None	

1   Description

The remark UoF provides the capability to annotate additional information relevant to the associated item which is not part of the immediate subject.

-   A key feature of the UoF remark data model is that a `Remark` can be associated with any class instance as well as with any individual attribute value. Refer to Fig 1.

2 UML class model

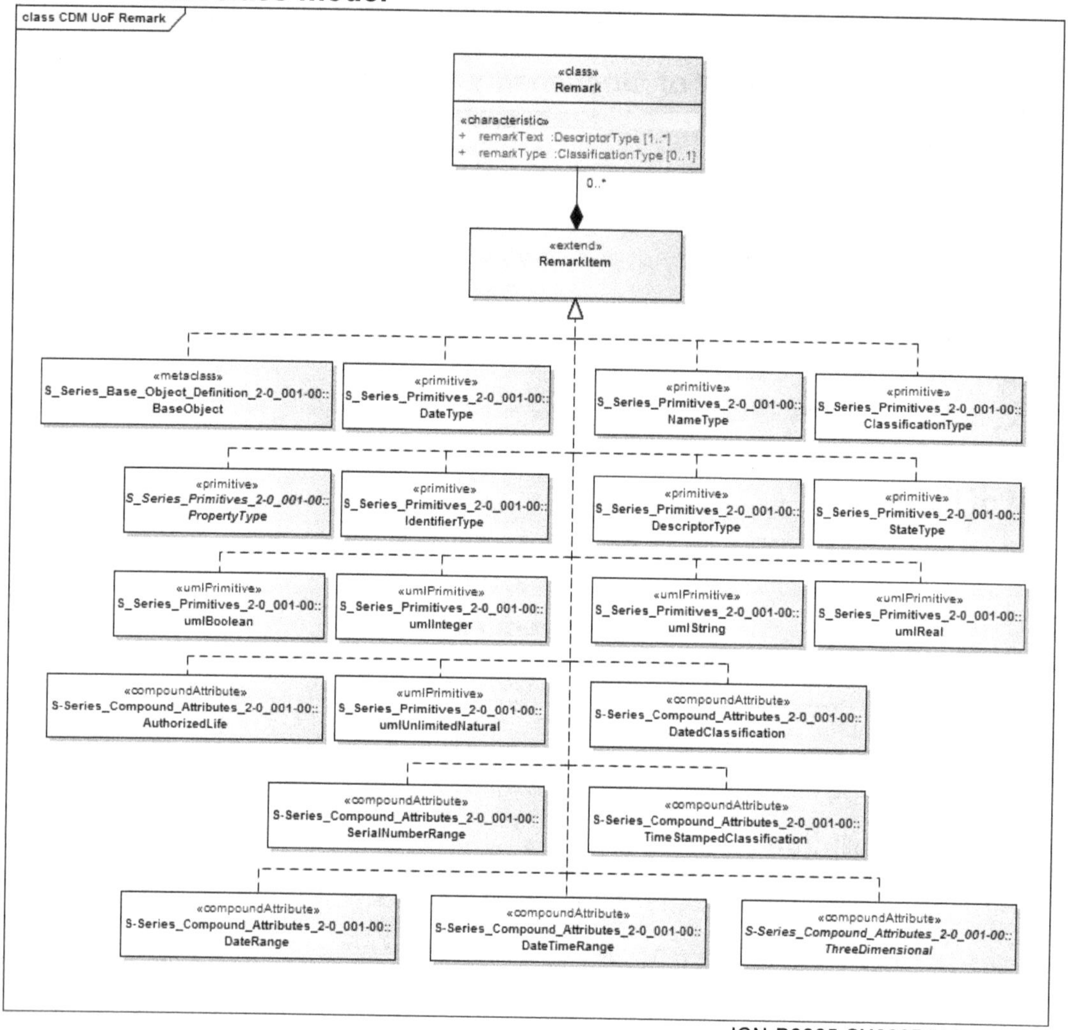

ICN-B6865-SX002D0022-002-01

Fig 1 UoF remark - UML class model

Chapter 3.33

Unit of functionality - Resource specification

Table of contents

List of tables

List of figures

References

Table 1 References

Chap No./Document No.	Title
Chap 3.26	SX002D-A-03-33-0000-00A-040A-A

1   Description

The resource specification UoF provides the capability to define generic definitions of resources needed, without having to define its actual realization.

Key features of the UoF resource specification data model (Refer to Fig 1) are:

- The type of `ResourceSpecification` defined is determined by the `resourceSpecificationType`
- A `ResourceSpecification` can be associated with one ore many `PartAsDesigned` (refer to Chap 3.26) that fulfills the specification

2   UML class model

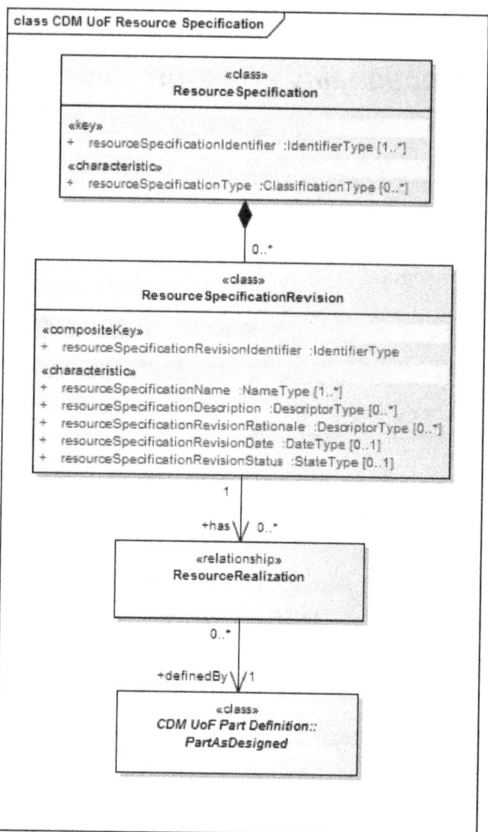

ICN-B6865-SX002D0058-001-01

Fig 1 UoF Resource specification - UML class model

Chapter 3.34

Unit of functionality - Security classification

Table of contents

List of tables

List of figures

References

Table 1 References

Chap No./Document No.	Title
None	

1 Description

The security classification UoF provides the capability to assign
`SecurityClassification`'s to objects that need special handling for protection
against unauthorized access or distribution.

2   UML class model

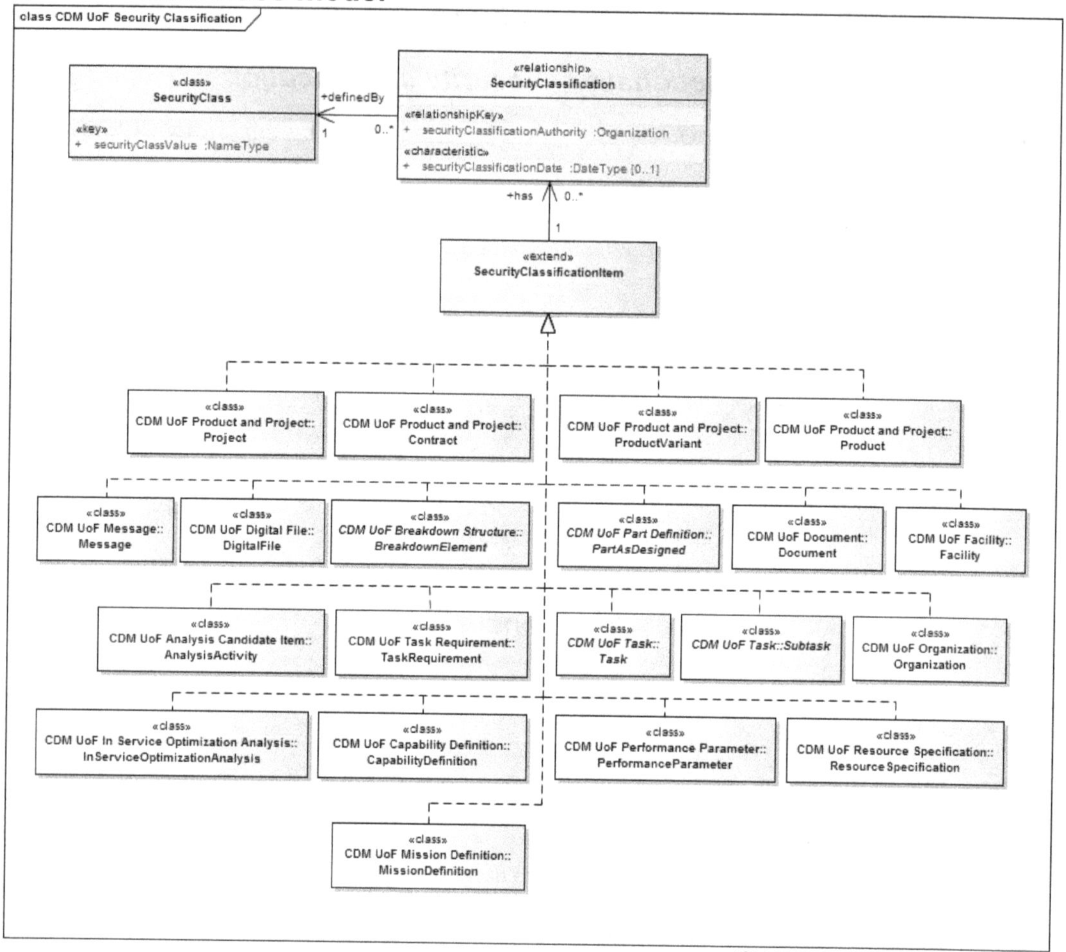

ICN-B6865-SX002D0010-003-01

Fig 1   UoF security classification - UML class model

Chapter 3.35

Unit of functionality - Serialized part configuration

Table of contents

List of tables

List of figures

References

Table 1 References

Chap No./Document No.	Title
Chap 3.25	Unit of functionality - Part as realized
Chap 3.26	Unit of functionality - Part definition
Chap 3.36	Unit of functionality - Serialized Product variant configuration

1   Description

The serialized part configuration UoF provides the capability to identify parts contained within a serialized part.

Key features of the UoF serialized part configuration data model (Refer to Fig 1) are:

- A `SerializedHardwarePart` (refer to Chap 3.25) should have one `SerializedPartsListPosition` for each corresponding `PartAsDesignedPartsListEntry` (refer to Chap 3.26) in the applicable `PartAsDesignedPartsList` defined for the `HardwarePartAsDesigned`
- The `InstalledPart` (refer to Chap 3.36) can either be a reference to a `SerializedHardwarePart`, a `BatchHardwarePart`, a `SoftwarePartAsRealized` (refer to Chap 3.25) or by reference to a `PartAsDesigned` (refer to Chap 3.26) where the part being installed is not tracked by serial or batch number

2   UML class model

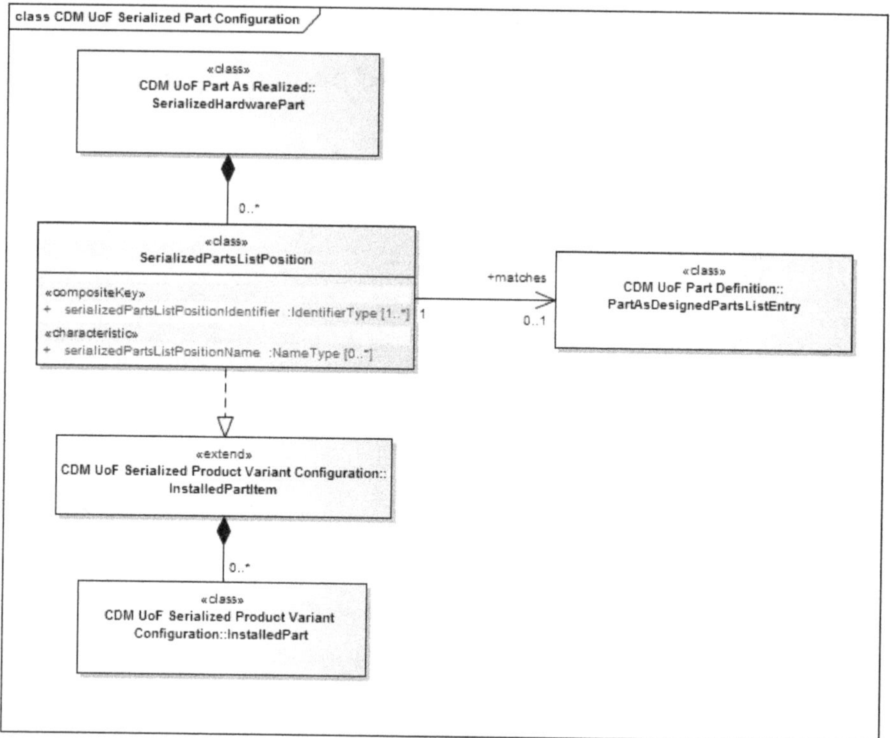

ICN-B6865-SX002D0039-004-01

Fig 1 UoF serialized part configuration - UML class model

Chapter 3.36

Unit of functionality - Serialized Product variant configuration

Table of contents

List of tables

List of figures

References

Table 1 References

Chap No./Document No.	Title
Chap 3.18	Unit of functionality - Hardware element
Chap 3.25	Unit of functionality - Part as realized
Chap 3.26	Unit of functionality - Part definition
Chap 3.28	Unit of functionality - Product and project
Chap 3.29	Unit of functionality - Product design configuration
Chap 3.37	Unit of functionality - Software element

1   Description

The serialized Product variant configuration UoF provides the capability to identify combinations of actual installation locations for a given serialized product variant and actual parts that are or have been installed at the respective installation location.

Key features of the UoF serialized Product variant configuration data model (Refer to Fig 1Fig 1) are:

- A `SerializedProductVariant` must always comply with one and only one `AllowedProductConfiguration` (refer to Chap 3.29) at any given point in time, but can comply with different `AllowedProductConfiguration`'s over time
- An `InstallationLocation` must always correspond to a `HardwareElement` (refer to Chap 3.18) or `SoftwareElement` (refer to Chap 3.37) in the breakdown for

the `ProductVariant` (refer to <u>Chap 3.28</u>) for which the `AllowedProductConfiguration` is defined
- The `InstalledPart` can either be a reference to a `SerializedHardwarePart`, a `BatchHardwarePart`, a `SoftwarePartAsRealized` (refer to <u>Chap 3.25</u>) or by reference to a `PartAsDesigned` (refer to <u>Chap 3.26</u>) where the part being installed is not tracked by serial or batch number

2   UML class model

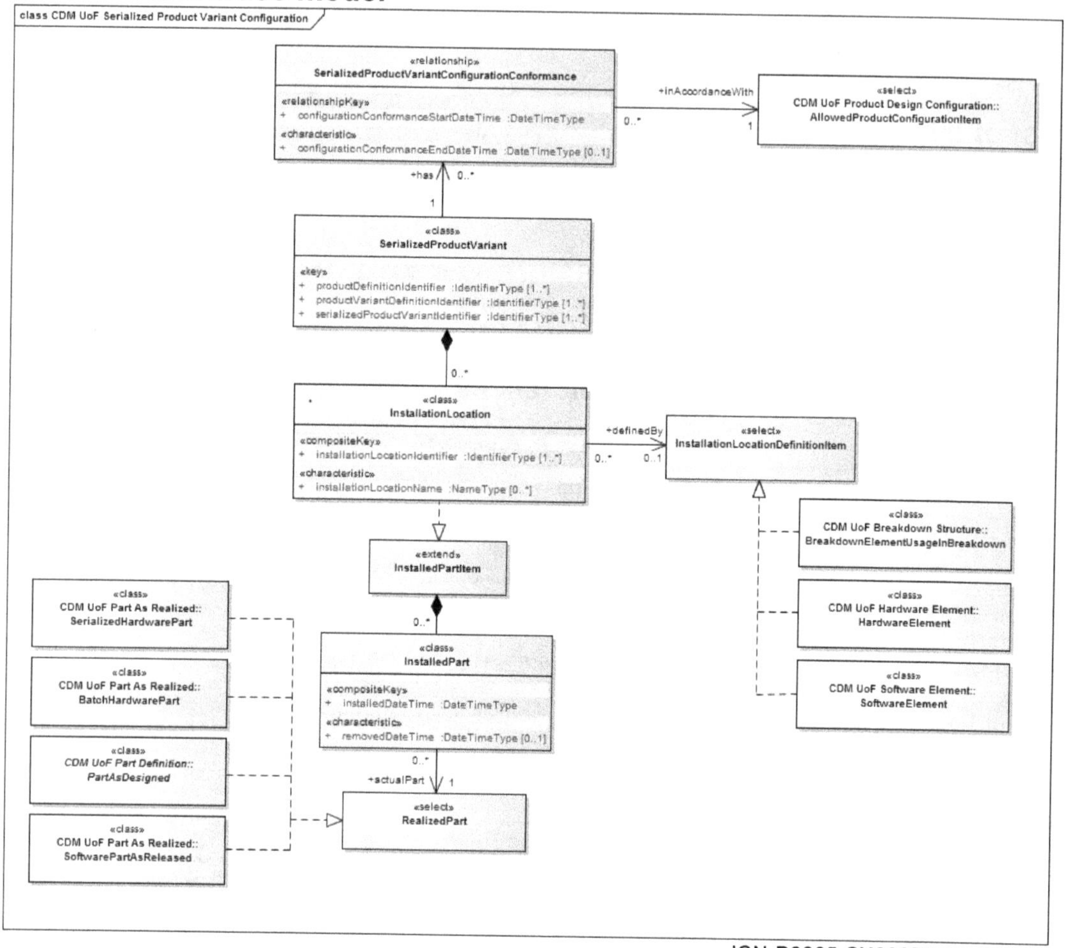

ICN-B6865-SX002D0040-005-01

Fig 1 UoF serialized Product variant configuration - UML class model

Chapter 3.37

Unit of functionality - Software element

Table of contents

List of tables

List of figures

References

Table 1 References

Chap No./Document No.	Title
Chap 3.5	Unit of functionality - Breakdown structure
Chap 3.26	Unit of functionality - Part definition

1 Description

The software element UoF provides the capability to specify that an element within a breakdown is software and can be associated with the software part(s) that fulfill the requirements.

Key features of the UoF software element data model (Refer to Fig 1) are:

- `SoftwareElement` is a specialization of `BreakdownElement` (refer to Chap 3.5) which means that, wherever `BreakdownElement` Is being used In the data model, `SoftwareElement` can be used instead
- `SoftwareElementRevision` is a specialization of `BreakdownElementRevision` which means that, wherever `BreakdownElementRevision` is being used in the data model, `SoftwareElement` Revision can be used instead
- An instance of `SoftwareElementRevision` can be associated with one or many instances of `SoftwarePartAsDesigned` (refer to Chap 3.26) that meet the requirements and specification for the `SoftwareElement`

2   UML class model

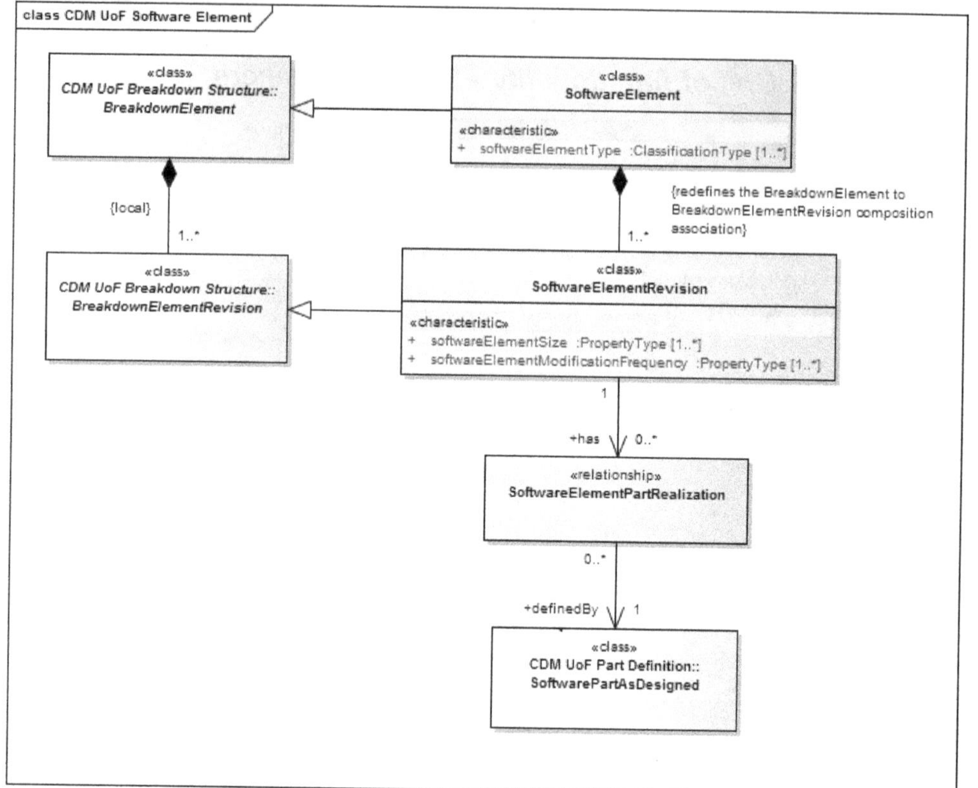

ICN-B6865-SX002D0006-004-01

Fig 1   UoF software element - UML class model

Chapter 3.38

Unit of functionality - Special event

Table of contents

List of tables

List of figures

References

Table 1 References

Chap No./Document No.	Title
Chap 3.3	Unit of functionality - Analysis candidate item
Chap 3.31	Unit of functionality - Product usage phase

1   Description

The special event UoF provides the capability to define typical happenings which can be induced to an item under analysis and which can impact the operational capability of the Product during its in service phase.

Key features of the UoF special event data model (Refer to Fig 1) are:

- `SpecialEventAnalysis` is a specialization of `AnalysisActivity` (refer to Chap 3.3) which means that `SpecialEventDefinition` is defined in the context of an `AnalysisCandidateItem`
- A `SpecialEventDefinition` can refer to a defined `ProductUsagePhase` during which the special event can occur (refer to Chap 3.31)

2 UML class model

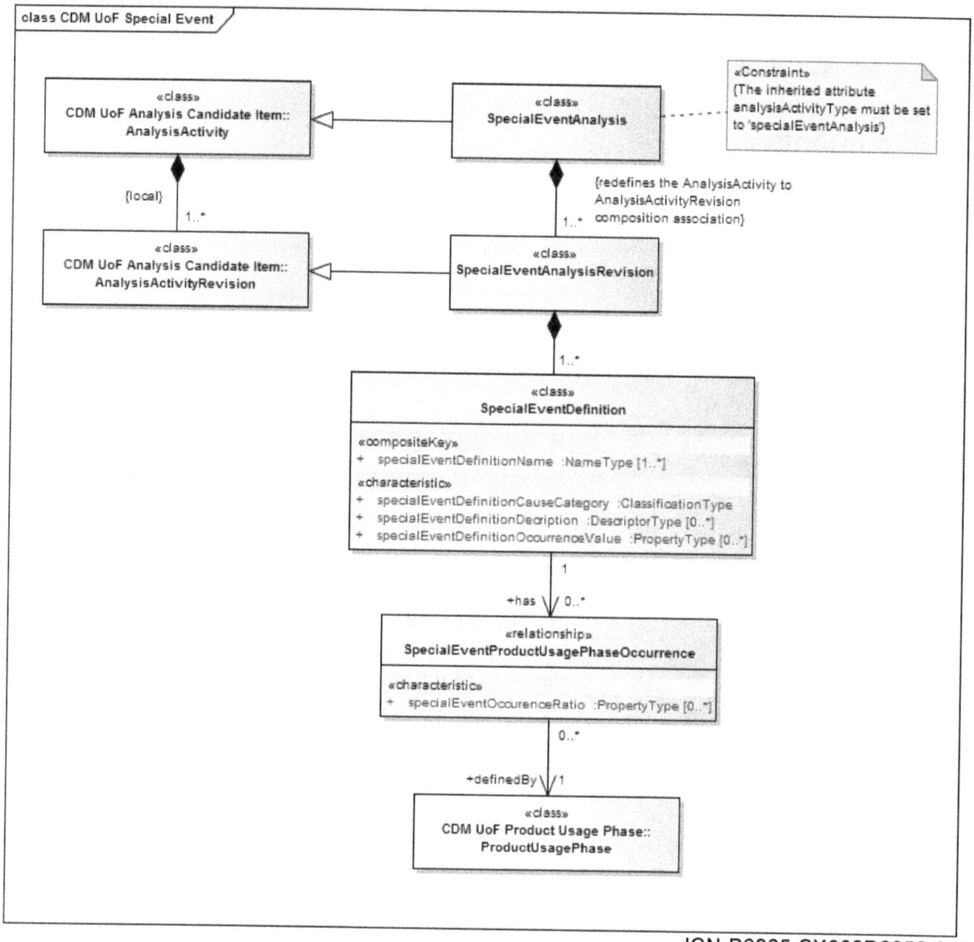

ICN-B6865-SX002D0059-001-01

Fig 1 UoF Special event - UML class model

Chapter 3.39

Unit of functionality - Task

Table of contents

List of tables

List of figures

References

Table 1 References

Chap No./Document No.	Title
Chap 3.28	Unit of functionality - Product and project
S1000D	International specification for technical publications using a common source database
S3000L	International procedure specification for Logistics Support Analysis (LSA)

1   Description

The task UoF supports the detailed definition of a task required to support a Product (refer to Chap 3.28).

Key features of the UoF task data model (Refer to Fig 1) are:

- A `Task` must be defined as either a `RectifyingTask`, `OperationalTask` or `SupportingTask`
- Work steps within a task, are described using a set of `Subtask`'s
- A `Subtask` can either be described in detail within the `Task` under consideration (`SubtaskByDefinition`) or by a reference to another `Task` (`SubtaskByTaskReference`)
- Time dependencies between `Subtask`'s can be defined using the `SubtaskTimeline` class. This can be used for the optimization of resource requirements and/or be the basis for, eg, creating job cards in a fleet management system

Note

A `SubtaskByDefinition`, which is defined and described within a `Task`, cannot be referenced by any other `Task`.

Note

The task UoF has been designed to support the integration between S3000L and the S1000D data module schemas for maintenance procedure and maintenance planning information, respectively.

2   UML class model

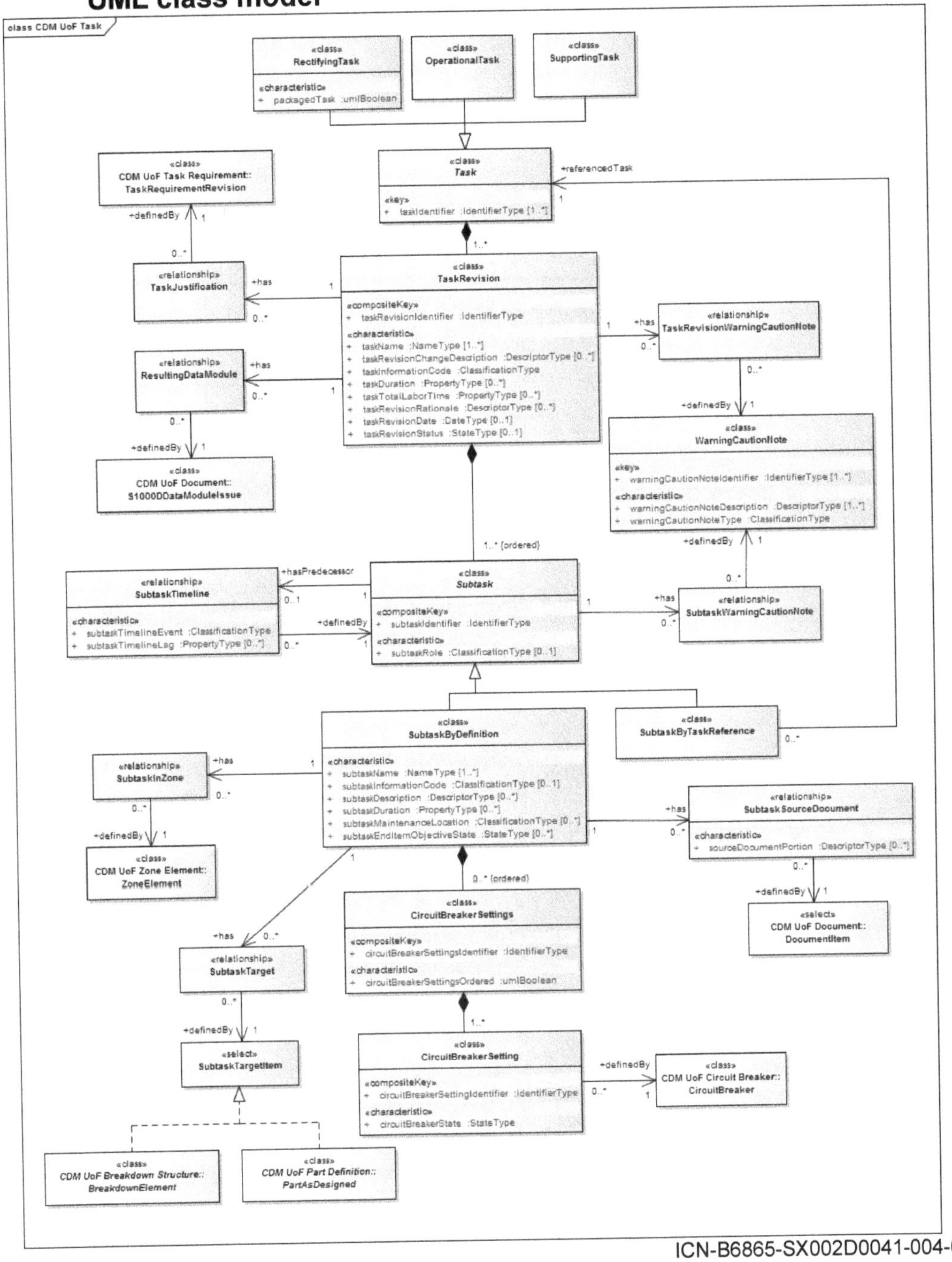

ICN-B6865-SX002D0041-004-01

Fig 1 UoF task - UML class model

Page intentionally blank.

Chapter 3.40

Unit of functionality - Task requirement

Table of contents

Page

List of tables

List of figures

References

Table 1 References

Chap No./Document No.	Title
Chap 3.5	Unit of functionality - Breakdown structure
Chap 3.26	Unit of functionality - Part definition
Chap 3.28	Unit of functionality - Product and project

1   Description

The task requirement UoF supports early documentation of the need for a task to be performed to support a `Product` (refer to Chap 3.28).

Note

An example on the objective for documenting `TaskRequirement`'s is to produce input to IPS review activities and to agree on maintenance concepts for the associated `BreakdownElementRevision` (refer to Chap 3.5) or `PartAsDesigned` (refer to Chap 3.26) before any detailed task analysis is carried out.

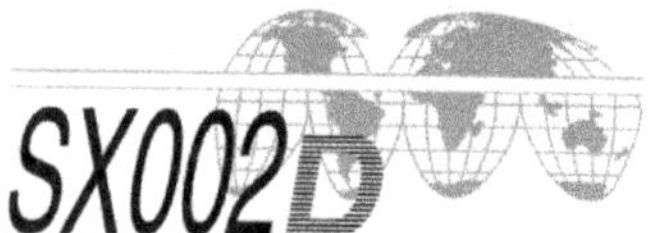

2 UML class model

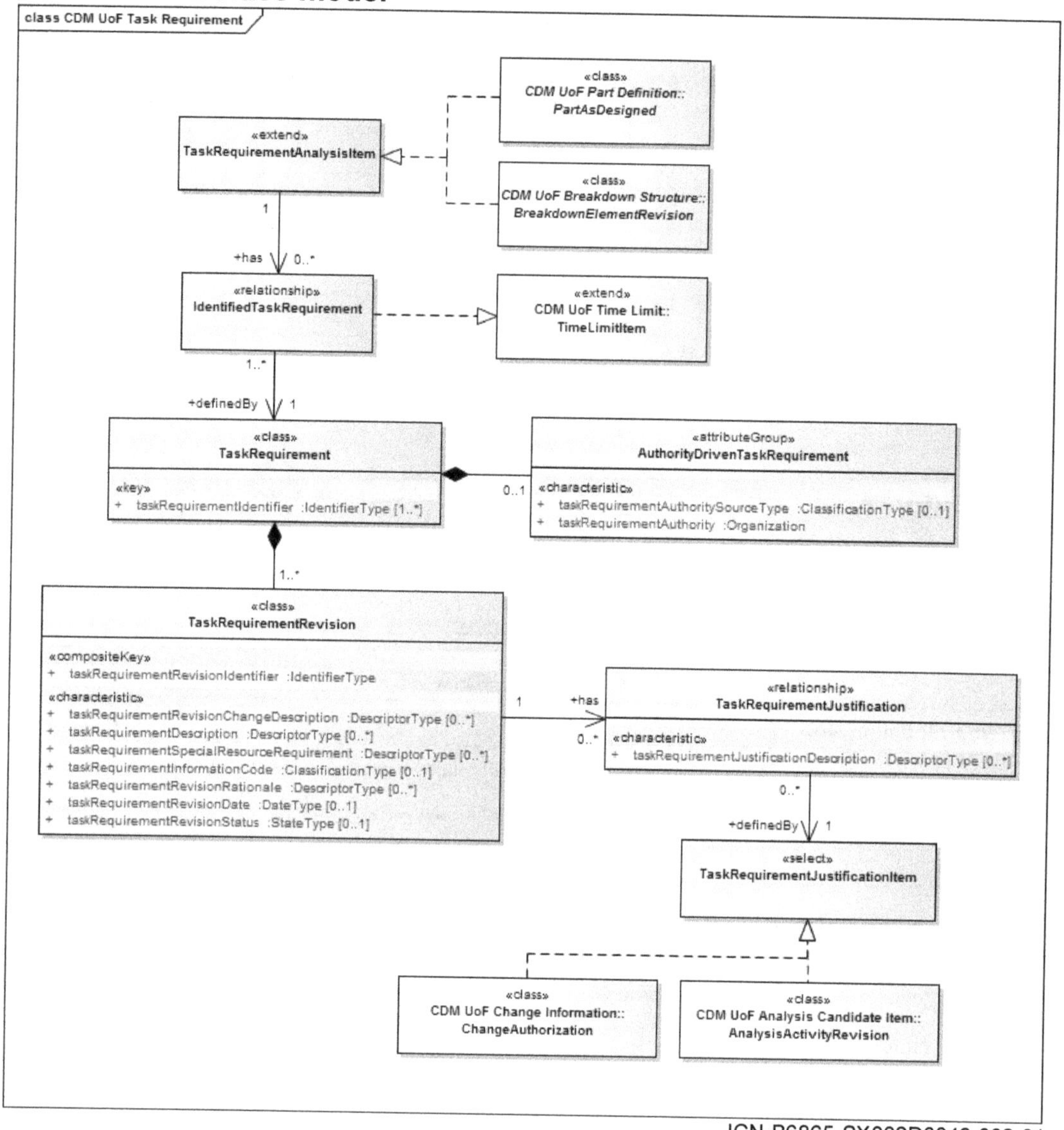

ICN-B6865-SX002D0042-002-01

Fig 1 UoF task requirement - UML class model

Chapter 3.41

Unit of functionality - Task resource

Table of contents

List of tables

List of figures

References

Table 1 References

Chap No./Document No.	Title
Chap 3.5	Unit of functionality - Breakdown structure
Chap 3.26	Unit of functionality - Part definition
Chap 3.33	Unit of functionality - Resource specification
Chap 3.39	Unit of functionality - Task

1   Description

The task resource UoF supports the detailed specification of resources needed to perform a specified amount of work.

Key features of the UoF task resource data model (Refer to Fig 1) are:

- A `TaskResource` can either be specified for the overall `Task` or per `Subtask` (refer to Chap 3.39)
- A `TaskResource` must be defined as either a:

  - `TaskMaterialResource` (eg, spare, tool, consumable, etc)
  - `TaskInfrastructureResource` (eg, hangar, power, etc)
  - `TaskPersonnelResource` (eg, skill, trade, etc)
  - `TaskDocumentResource` (eg, forms for recording test results)

- `TaskMaterialResource` and `TaskInfrastructureResource` can be defined in terms of:

- `ResourceSpecification` (refer to Chap 3.33)
- `BreakdownElement` (refer to Chap 3.5)
- `PartAsDesigned` (refer to Chap 3.26)
- `PartAsDesignedPartsListEntry` (refer to Chap 3.26)

2   UML class model

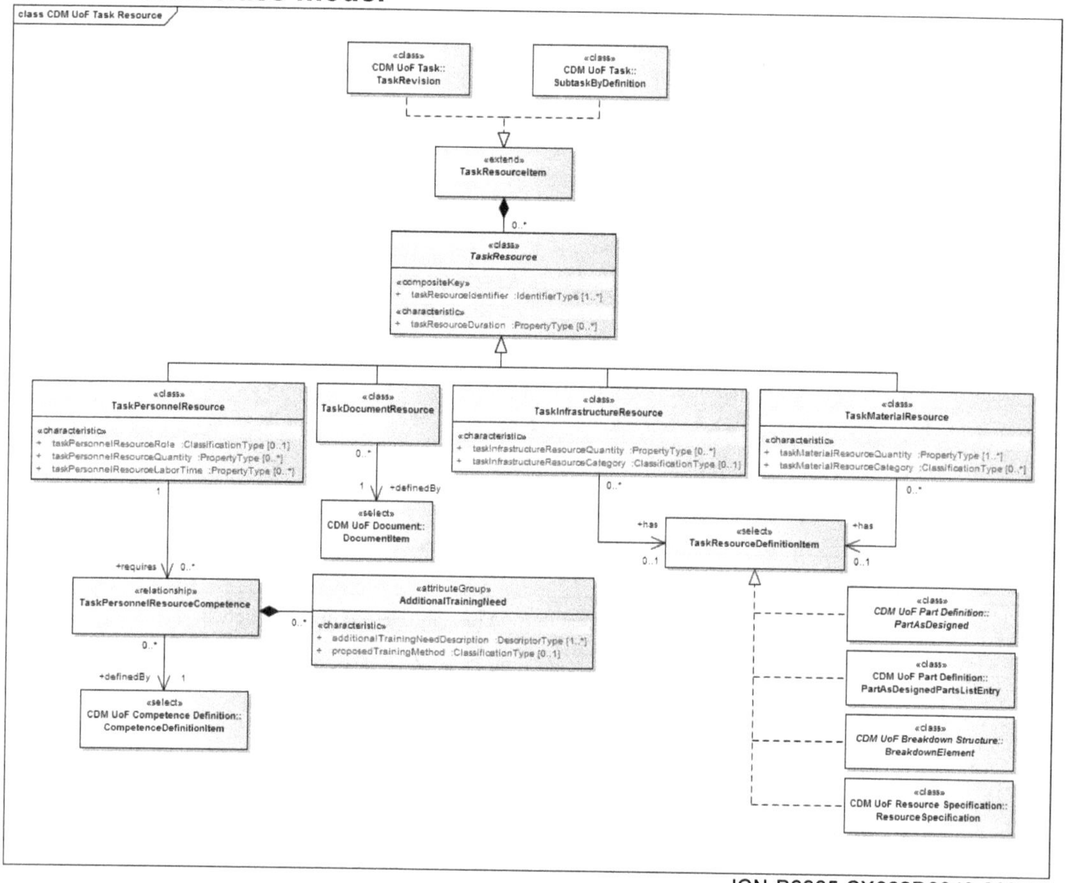

ICN-B6865-SX002D0043-002-01

Fig 1   UoF task resource - UML class model

Chapter 3.42

Unit of functionality - Task usage

Table of contents

List of tables

List of figures

References

Table 1 References

Chap No./Document No.	Title
Chap 3.5	Unit of functionality - Breakdown structure
Chap 3.26	Unit of functionality - Part definition
Chap 3.39	Unit of functionality - Task

1   Description

The task usage UoF provides capability to expand the definition for the execution of a task in the context of a given support solution.

Key features of the UoF task usage data model (Refer to Fig 1) are:

- Identifies the `BreakdownElementRevision` (refer to Chap 3.5) or `PartAsDesigned` (refer to Chap 3.26) on which the associated `Task` (refer to Chap 3.39) is to be performed
- Can define the frequency for the associated `Task`
- Can define where the associated `Task` is to be performed in the context of a given support solution

2 UML class model

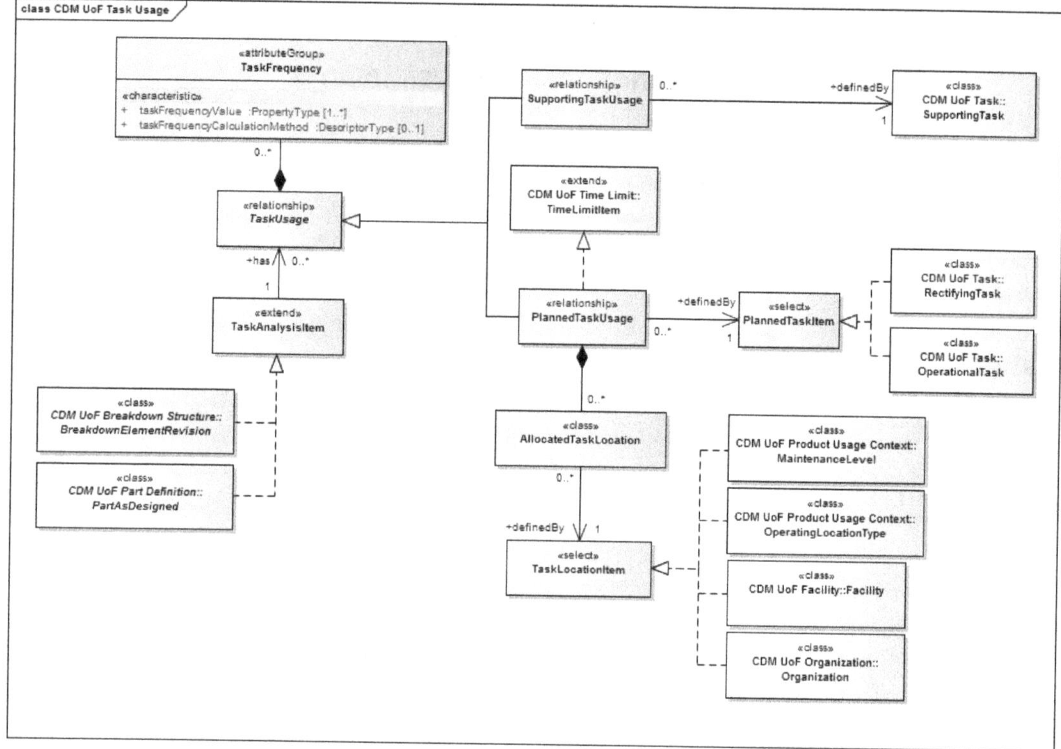

ICN-B6865-SX002D0044-002-01

Fig 1 UoF task usage - UML class model

Chapter 3.43

Unit of functionality - Time limit

Table of contents

List of tables

List of figures

References

Table 1 References

Chap No./Document No.	Title
None	

1   Description

The time limit UoF provides the capability to define the circumstances under which an action is to be initiated.

Key features of the UoF time limit data model (Refer to Fig 1) are:

- A `TimeLimit` must be defined as either a `DiscreteTimeLimit` where its next possible occurrence cannot be scheduled or, as a `PeriodicTimeLimit`, where the associated action is to be repeated and its next occurrence can be scheduled
- The `trigger` and/or `threshold` that initiates the action can either be defined by a parameter value or be associated with a specific event

2   UML class model

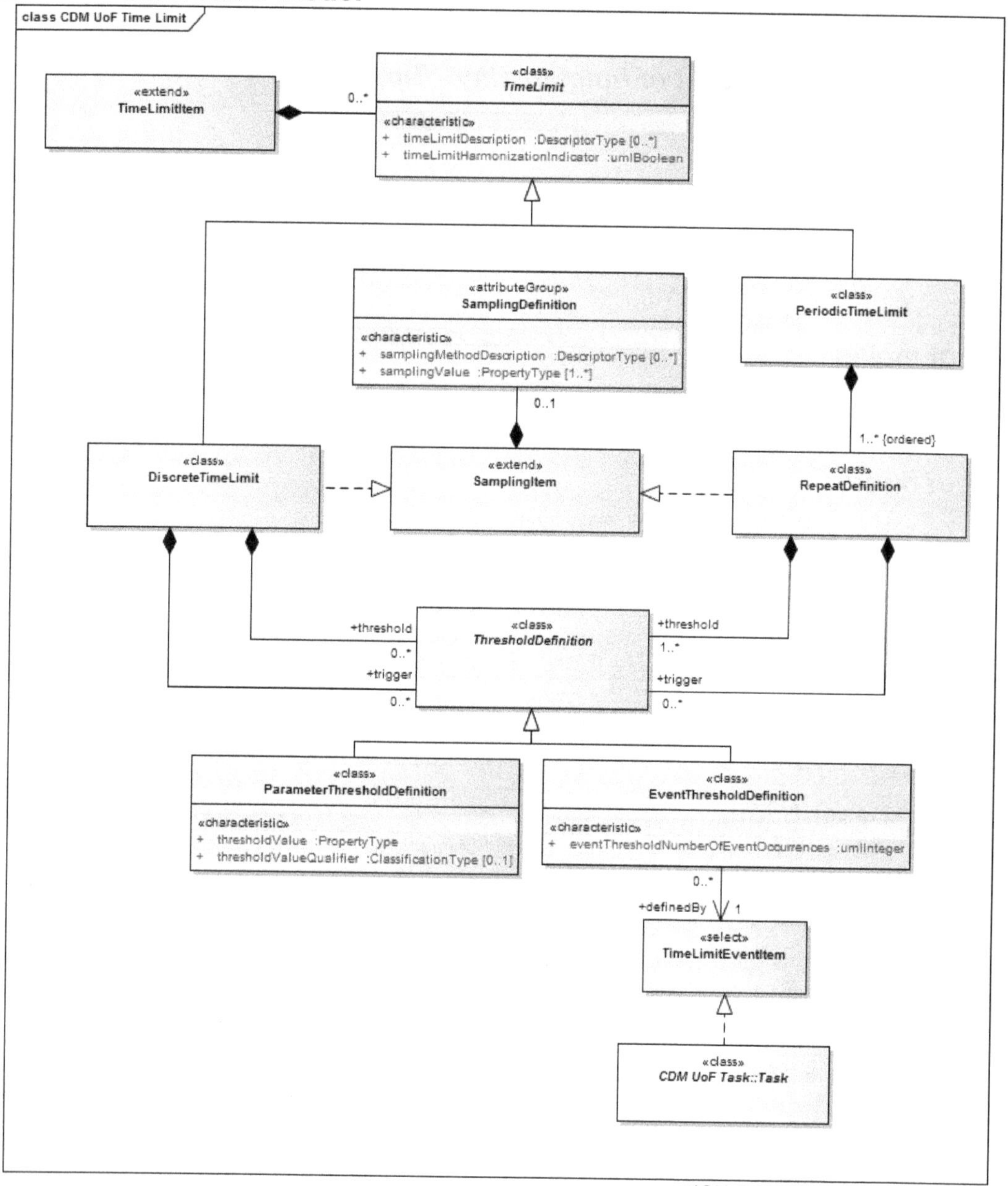

ICN-B6865-SX002D0045-002-01

Fig 1   UoF time limit - UML class model

Chapter 3.44

Unit of functionality - Zone element

Table of contents

List of tables

List of figures

References

Table 1 References

Chap No./Document No.	Title
Chap 3.5	Unit of functionality - Breakdown structure
Chap 3.28	Unit of functionality - Product and project

1   Description

The zone element UoF defines the characteristics that are unique for a `BreakdownElement` (refer to Chap 3.5) which represents a three-dimensional space related to a `Product` (refer to Chap 3.28).

Key features of the UoF zone element data model (Refer to Fig 1) are:

- `ZoneElement` is a specialization of `BreakdownElement` which means that, wherever `BreakdownElement` is being used in the data model, `ZoneElement` or can be used instead
- `ZoneElementRevision` is a specialization of `BreakdownElementRevision` which means that, wherever `BreakdownElementRevision` is being used in the data model, `ZoneElementRevision` can be used instead
- An instance of `ZoneElement` can have one or more associated `BreakdownElements` (including specific revisions and usages thereof) which are located in the three-dimensional space that the `ZoneElement` represents.

2　UML class model

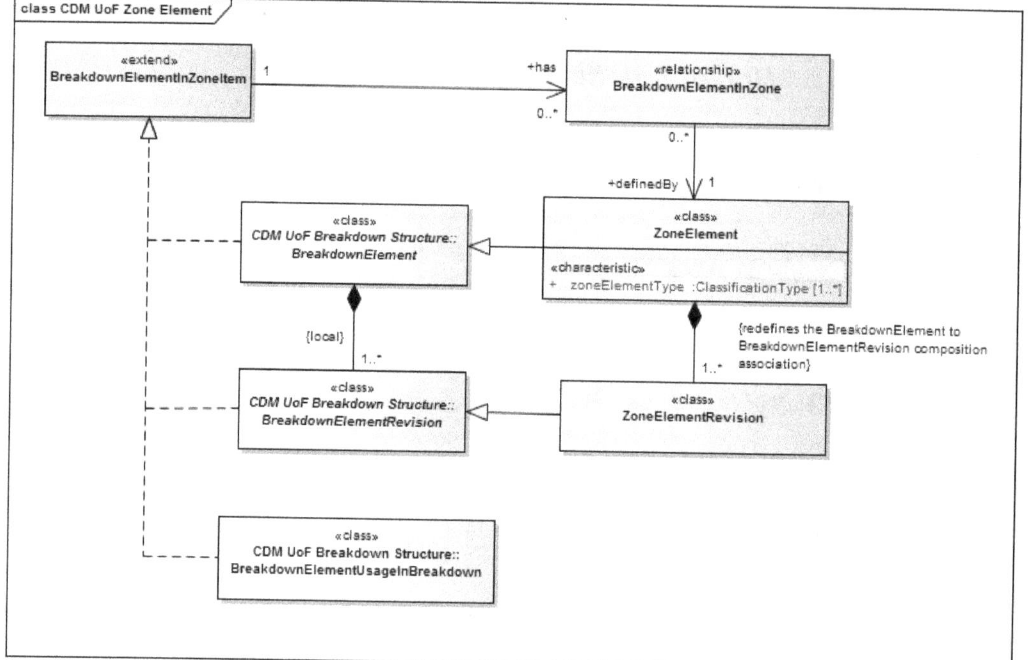

ICN-B6865-SX002D0007-004-01

Fig 1　UoF zone element - UML class model